Luther Boutelle

Sketch of the Life and Religious Experience of Eld. Luther Boutelle

Luther Boutelle

Sketch of the Life and Religious Experience of Eld. Luther Boutelle

ISBN/EAN: 9783337258863

Printed in Europe, USA, Canada, Australia, Japan

Cover: Foto ©ninafisch / pixelio.de

More available books at **www.hansebooks.com**

SKETCH OF THE LIFE

AND

RELIGIOUS EXPERIENCE

OF

ELD. LUTHER BOUTELLE.
WRITTEN BY HIMSELF.

WITH AN INTRODUCTION BY
WILLIAM H. MITCHELL.

PUBLISHED FOR THE AUTHOR
BY THE
ADVENT CHRISTIAN PUBLICATION SOCIETY,
144 HANOVER ST., BOSTON.
1891.

PREFACE.

To the readers of this book. The author of these pages would say, that not until recently were they contemplated, and this only by the desire of friends, who urgently requested that something of the kind be written by me.

As I had kept no journal of my life-experience, I have had to depend upon my memory in giving this narrative. I have given only a glimpse of the way along down to the present time.

The goodness of God has been manifested during all my life, and I wish it might have been more set forth in these pages. This I have attempted to show: the special care that God has for those who trust him, and do his will. Also the regard he has for the accomplishment of his word, and the keeping of his promises.

In sending forth this imperfect sketch of my lengthened life, my prayer is that it may be for the glory of God and the strengthening and comforting of all who read these pages.

L. BOUTELLE.

Chelsea, Mass.

INTRODUCTION.

Books have their influence, and therefore leave their impress on the human mind. Some have a very debasing effect; others elevate and refine. The lives of good men have a very healthy influence upon society, hence a record of the incidents and events of their lives wherein God hath wrought graciously with them is valuable to preserve. The wise man saith, "The memory of the just is blessed."

Who does not feel that he is made better by reading the lives of great and good men? When Paul wrote to the Hebrew church he related some of the wonderful events in the lives of the suffering saints of God. When the king of Israel was holding converse with the servant of the prophet Elisha, he desired him to tell him all the great things that "Elisha did." So like the king when we hear of men of eminent piety we desire to know something of their religious experience.

More than a quarter of a century has passed since I became acquainted with the author of this narrative, and our frequent interviews and correspondence have been so pleasant, that I have often thought a brief narrative of his life and religious experience written by himself, together with many of his excellent articles published in years past, might make a book which would be both interesting and profitable to the religious body with which he has long been connected, as well as his numerous friends.

A few months ago I suggested to him I should be pleased to have such a book to place in my library. The thought struck him at first unfavorably at the advanced age of his life, the task seeming too much for him to undertake; but, upon more mature reflection he consented to undertake the work, and now this little volume is completed and sent forth to greet the thousands of his friends and acquaintances with whom he has mingled in years past, and to whom he has faithfully preached the unsearchable riches of Christ, and heralded the speedy advent of the Messiah.

In conclusion, I would say, I hope this little book will find a hearty welcome among the household of faith, cheering, comforting and instructing, like its author during his minstry of the word of God among his fellowmen.

W. H. MITCHELL.

Kennebunk, Maine, Nov. 5th, 1890.

CONTENTS.

	PAGE.
Preface	iii
Introduction	iv

CHAPTER I.
Parentage, Birth and Early Life.................... 9

CHAPTER II.
Later in Life—Choice of Occupation.................. 15

CHAPTER III.
Married and Settled in Life........................ 19

CHAPTER IV.
Conviction and Conversion.......................... 24

CHAPTER V.
United with the Church............................ 29

CHAPTER VI.
A Strange Sound—New Subject...................... 38

CHAPTER VII.
Leaving Home to Give the Message.................. 45

CHAPTER VIII.
Returning Home, Incidents......................... 56

CHAPTER IX.
Great Interest in the Coming of Christ............... 62

CHAPTER X.
The Great Disappointment.......................... 65

CHAPTER XI.
Resuming the Work with Good Courage.............. 71

CHAPTER XII.
Still Pressing on in the Work......................... 77

CHAPTER XIII.
Changes, with a New Time........................... 83

CHAPTER XIV.
Experience and Deep Affliction....................... 88

CHAPTER XV.
Sick, Miraculously Healed............................ 92

CHAPTER XVI.
Health Restored. A Neighbor Quieted............... 99

CHAPTER XVII.
Healing in Answer to Prayer......................... 112

CHAPTER XVIII.
Afflicted with Loss of Hearing....................... 118

CHAPTER XIX.
Death in family. Visit to Vernon, Vt................ 123

MISCELLANEOUS.
I. Divine Healing............................ 128
II. Is Christ's Coming Near?................. 138
III. A Tremendous Lie........................ 143
IV. Thy Kingdom Come...................... 145
V. Spiritual Longevity....................... 148
VI. Pastoral Resignations.................... 150

VIII.	The Prayer of Jesus..................	154
IX.	Strikes...............................	155
X.	And Knew Not.......................	157
XI.	Reverend.............................	161
XII.	A Tour In Connecticut...............	163
XIII.	Care of the Watchman...............	165
XIV.	Retrospect of Forty Years............	167
XV.	Apostasy.............................	169
XVI.	Life Like a Dream...................	171
XVII.	A Hard Case.........................	173
XVIII.	An Eye Opener.......................	175
XIX.	Hard Experience.....................	177
XX.	My Pilgrimage.......................	179
XXI.	Materialism...........................	181
XXII.	Old Landmarks.......................	183
XXIII.	The Good Fight of Faith.............	184
XXIV.	He that Shall Endure to the End.....	185
XXV.	Caution..............................	187
XXVI.	Wisdom at an End—Truth Mighty....	189
XXVII.	New Departure......................	193
XXVIII.	Back There..........................	196
XXIX.	No Scars Left........................	198
XXX.	Beecher Dead........................	200
XXXI.	Did Jesus Die?.......................	201
XXXII.	A Sermon............................	204

CHAPTER I.

Parentage, Birth and Early Life.

MY honored parents were born in Reading, Mass. My mother's maiden name was Abagail Bancroft, daughter of James Bancroft, Esq. After my father's and mother's marriage they moved to West Boylston, Mass., from thence to Townsend, where they died; my mother at eighty-three years, and my father within a few days of ninety-four. They were among the most devoted Christians.

I was born in Townsend, May 4, 1806. My father was known as Deacon John Boutelle. He and my mother were among the respectable people of the town, and in the common condition of life. There were nine children of us, but four died before I was born, and it was by the strictest economy and unrelaxed industry that my parents supported the family. My father got his living mainly by shoemaking. In those times there was but little money in the country, and the most that my father earned he had to take in produce. In those days it was necessary for all, in the common condition of life, to work hard; and it took both brain and physical strength to keep a family in food and clothing, especially if the family was large. Thus frugality and diligence in daily life then were among the first lessons we children had to learn.

The district school was the only place of learning that the common people then had; and this was only held from three to five months in the year. There were no high schools in those days, from which poor children could graduate. If we could be spared from work to attend all the time that the district school was kept, we were fortunate indeed, a privilege to be greatly prized. The winter session of the school was especially the harvest of knowledge. But if one wanted a nice send-off in his teens, he must be sent to the minister a short time for the "finishing touch," which would fit him for a teacher of the district school.

In those stubborn times, when we had to utilize with energy our time and strength to get a living, working "in the sweat of the face," there were no amusements or holidays for the young as now. The fourth of July and "muster day" were all we boys could anticipate for recreation and pleasure; and these without money to spend for nicknacks. The pennies then came hard, and not many could the children get to buy what they liked. This was the case especially with the children of Deacon John Boutelle. But what they lacked in spending-money was more than made up in good instruction, which is a better foundation than riches. We were taught to be strictly honest, and to adhere closely to the "Puritan religion, brought over in the May Flower." This gave us children our moral start-off. Punctuality at meeting was among our first lessons. It was, "Come, boys and girls, be ready; the first bell is ringing." Excuses availed nothing. If the old folks could go, the children could as well. So when health prevailed the three miles' walk to the meeting house was constant every Sabbath, besides a supplement now and then on week-days. Only to do as required—that was all that was to be done by us children. Parental government was then in vogue, and to exercise parental authority was obligatory on every parent. Children were not as disobedient to parents and teachers then as now. There was reverence for the old then, and it was manifested at all times by well-bred children.

My father had a small farm, and so we kept a cow and hog, with some hens. These needed looking after; and this was done by us boys as soon as we could well stir about out of doors. My father worked in his shop all the time except in planting and harvest times. With what we children could do, helping him and our mother, the family lived and were as happy as families now are that have wealth and all that they desire, with no labor or care. Our childhood and youth soon passed. We had good neighbors of the same way of living; so there was no envy, jealousy or strife. All were ready to help one another. There was then a link that kept people together, especially in the country. Honest, hard-working farmers, the most of them, they were more bound to each other than any other class of men. In sickness or adversity of any kind, there was sympathy and help given. In those times it was not unfashionable to have a large family of children. Then the marriage state was entered into with the expectation of having a family. This was God's arrangement at the beginning of the race, and he has made no change in his plan and law. The birth of children in my early days was a matter for rejoicing in the family, neighborhood and town. No matter if the family was poor, the neighbors did not say, "Oh dear! there is another mouth to feed! What a pity!" With people then, it was God that gave. Children make an oasis in the desert of life.

Barren, fruitless trees may be worth something for shade; but trees full of fruit delight the eye, and cheer those who eat thereof. A family without children (if it can be called a family) is a domestic desolation. But such was not the family of Deacon John Boutelle.

Thus we came along in the battle of life under good instruction, which for us was worth more than wealth with no teaching of righteousness, or example of holy living. What we got as we grew up we prized, and were quite contented with it. Our *needs* were mostly supplied. Good health-giving food and warm clothing we did not lack, though the latter was not so fine as children now wear. The children in those days had the advantage of the children now. There were not then the temptations, the allurements to evil that now are found everywhere, drawing the young away from virtue to vice. There were no confection shops where the young could go and get rid of their pennies and their health. Whole families grew up without having toys, or playthings, only such as they contrived themselves. It was then a good time to bring up children. They were more contented at home than abroad. Fashions did not change very often. If you got your winter outfit by Thanksgiving, of cotton and wool, spun, wove, and made up at home; with new shoes or boots, they would do for the children all winter, for meeting, school, or anywhere else, provided the wearers were careful at home and in their play.

Thus the good old ways of almost a century ago had a better look for the peace, prosperity and happiness in domestic life than this age. There was then a general satisfaction with all the surroundings; a prevailing interest among all your neighbors in your prosperity and welfare; and which united them, as a community, in the closest friendship. They were well acquainted with one another's joys and sorrows.

CHAPTER II.

Later in Life—Choice of Occupation.

HAVING come into our teens, an outlook for ourselves was the thing first in order, and which interested us all; for the homestead must be left. The bees must swarm, and where will they light? This is an important question in youth. A decision must be made as to the way one is to gain a livelihood. Some occupation must be chosen, some business engaged in by which to live. So the three boys, Luther, Calvin and Ebenezer had to decide what to do. Luther and Calvin were twins, while Ebenezer was four years younger. Calvin went to learn the carpenter's trade. My health being poor, I stayed about home, doing what I could that came to hand, working out from home as I found what I could do. It was a strong desire of my parents that one of their sons should become a minister. Especially it was the wish of my father that Ebenezer should be fitted for evangelical work. But the means of preparing him to preach, by sending him through the schools, was not at hand. Going through academies and colleges cost more than Deacon John Boutelle had to spend on his son Ebenezer. So contentment was the best thing to exercise. The common country schools were all that could be looked to by the poor people for education. Ebenezer gave up being a minister, and went to be a carpenter. As for myself, I did not aspire to scholastic wisdom, although I could learn easily. With little study I could keep up with the rest in the school, and this was satisfactory all around. The finishing touch to my education was given by our minister, the Rev. David Palmer. My twin brother also was under his tuition a few weeks at the same time. Here we "graduated." Then I was ready to teach school, or engage in any other vocation as the way opened.

While at home, I had become accustomed to the use of shoe tools, and could work well with them. In the meantime I had tried another occupation; but did not make out very well in it. At length there was an opening for me to go into the shoe business at Groton, Mass.

Now I will say what may be more important. While we, as a family, were all at home, we attended one and the same meeting. There were then few divisions among religionists. All that wanted pure and undefiled religion could have this one kind, which was apostolic. Then one meeting-house and one minister would do for the whole town. The church and people did not get tired of the minister as quickly as now. They did not want so many new things as do the people of this day. If the minister preached some of his sermons over the second and third time, the hearers found no fault. There was order in every thing then. The church helped to carry out the laws of the State. One thing I will mention, which in those days seemed to be very important. When a couple in the town were engaged to be married, the marriage certificate must be seen three Sundays in succession in the "information-box" at the meeting-house, and be cried by the town clerk on each Sunday. If this was not done the msrriage would not be lawful. In those days couples did not privately slip away into other towns, or to the city, and come back and say they were married. That would not have done then.

The minister in those times was supposed to know every thing. He was sound in politics, in theology and all doctrines. The isms were not as numerous as now. Strong Bible preaching, the prayer meeting and Sunday meeting—these for the whole town were enough to save the perishing then; so it was thought. All seemed satisfied, as nearly all attended meeting. It was looked upon as heathenish to stay away from the Sunday meeting. Even if it did rain, that would not be a good and sufficient reason for absence. Nothing but sickness would answer for an excuse for not being in the house of God on his holy day. The births and deaths were announced from the pulpit before the morning service, and devout prayer was offered appropriate to each case. Thus a general knowledge was had of events transpiring in the town. No Sunday papers then; no places of amusement or recreation. No going here and there for pleasure. All at home—it was the Sabbath. The people were hospitable, charitable, kind, and had an interest in one another, not separated by sectarianism or different creeds, with bigotry, which is the result of party religion. Instead of oyster suppers, fairs and sociables, by which to raise money to pay the minister's salary, they gave freely according as they had means, and so there were no church entertainments, no gambling to support the gospel. What was needed to sustain the good cause of the Master was readily found, for the people of the town were all interested in having good, wholesome instruction given to young and old. Minister and people were the one class. Equality was regarded and felt. Religion was acknowledged as needful by those who did not possess it.

CHAPTER III.

Marriage and Settled in Life.

I WAS about sixteen years old when it became necessary for me to decide upon having some permanent employment. It was about this time that my brother Calvin, as I have before said, went away to learn the carpenter's trade. But while I was trying to determine what to select as my occupation, I still remained at home working there or near home, as work presented itself, helping my father in the shop at times, as did my brother Ebenezer. But at length, in March, 1825, I went to Groton, Mass., and engaged to work for Loring Gates, in his shoe shop. This was my first leaving home permanently, a father's house and parental care. I soon got into my employer's favor, and here I was a long time. I often visited home and parents. Having become acquainted with Miss Hannah Conant, an attachment sprang up between us, and our union was agreed upon; and on the 14th day of August, 1830, we were married. The ceremony took place at Solomon Green's, in Townsend, on "Baybary Hill;" the Rev. David Palmer officiating, in the presence of parents and relatives. After a lunch and many congratulations, we left, with friends in three other carriages, for our chosen home in Groton. On our arrival we were welcomed by a party of friends at our new home in the house of Mr. John Peabody, on the corner facing Groton common. Here I commenced to learn my first lessons in domestic life. Here was my home until 1865. I was twenty-four years of age when married, but on account of poor health I had laid up nothing. This prevented me from marrying before I did. But at length I concluded that nothing was gained by waiting, and poverty should never stand in the way of having a wife—that a man was only a half an one without a wife. I made up my mind to run the risk of beginning this new life, and I was never sorry that I took the step. I had friends in my native town and in the one I had chosen for my residence. I had better views of life after I began it in God's order.

My brother Calvin married before I did, and settled down in Townsend on the Deacon Giles' place. A little time after Ebenezer found an amiable young women in Lowell by the name of Sarah Richardson, and they were married. My sister, Abigail Boutelle, had sometime before married a man by the name of Zela Bartlett. They lived in Springfield, Vt. This left only my sister Sally Boutelle, unmarried, with the old folks; so that in 1830, we all had got our way apparently laid out, with the battle of life fully begun, and some of us having had additions along the way. My first child was born 1831. This increased my responsibility, and added to my anxiety as to supporting a family.

I had before this taken great interest in the then new doctrine of total abstinence from all intoxicating drinks. I was interested in the movement at the time the old "Ironclad" was brought into Salem harbor, and fired the first bomb-shell into Deacon Giles' distillery, which made a mighty stir, and caused some legal threatening, if nothing more. There was great excitement at this time in regard to this new movement of temperance. I did what I could to keep it up. Then came the slavery question. The horrors of slavery pictured out by Mr. Lloyd Garrison stirred up the whole country. I at once became an Abolitionist, and identified myself with the haters of slavery. I did not go to the extreme of pronouncing every one a hypocrite who did not go in for the liberation of the slaves at once.

Some could not see that this would be best, if it could be done.

During all these years I made no profession of religion, and for the reason, that I had none to profess. I was all the time a church-going man, found among the singers at all the meetings. When I first came to Groton there was only one meeting, the Rev. Dr. Champlin's. He was the town's minister. But soon, on account of age he became unable to preach, and a division took place in the church, the Orthodox part withdrawing, leaving the Unitarian part in possession of the house. At this time there was a strife between the radical Congregationalists and the liberal Unitarians generally, and finally a complete separation took place. Those who withdrew built themselves a new meeting-house. The corner stone was laid July 4, 1826. I was present at the ceremony of laying the stone, and helped in the singing. The Rev. John Todd became the pastor, and preached the dedication sermon. In this division, I took the Orthodox side with youthful vigor, although unconverted. About this time I removed to the house of William Rowe, lived there a while, working at shoes in the shop of Cragin & Company. A little later I bought a house, put up and covered by John Hartwell. This was fitted up by finishing the inside myself, and soon as it was possible, moved into it; seeming there to begin life anew. Now a home of my own, a place I could call mine. How different from all others; where my wife could step out and walk around upon our own soil and not feel that it belonged to somebody else. Here we had born to us twins. We named them Augustus and Augusta. They were born May 23, 1837. This was quite an addition to our family, but it added to our stock of happiness, as well as to our cares. We grew happier and happier as the changes in life came.

CHAPTER IV.

Conviction and Conversion.

OUR home soon became an antislavery hotel. Here Mr. Garrison, Oliver Johnson, Fred Douglas and other leading antislavery men came; for Groton had become a noted place for abolition agitation, and my hand and heart were in it. Antislavery meetings were often held, and the abolition ball was kept rolling. Wm. L. Chaplin lived near me. He with Dr. Farnsworth and others, a goodly number, were awake on the subject, and were hated by the pro-slavery people all around. The history of this time is memorable. When George Thompson, of England, came to visit the New England abolitionists, we had a great meeting for his reception. It was held in the Congregational meeting-house. Such a meeting could not be held in Boston, there was so much hatred of him. He came and was welcomed by a crowded house. His first speech in this country was made in Groton. He was the guest of Dr. Farnsworth. That meeting was one of great interest. These were exciting times. Antislavery men were put to the test for courage and patience. They had the backs of former friends turned on them. I remember that the evening after Mr. Garrison had given us a lecture in Groton, of taking him over to Townsend where he was also to speak. The lecture was to be in the Congregational house. So I thought, as I drove into town, I would call on the minister, as the meeting was to be in his house. I drove directly to the door in order to give him an introduction to Mr. Garrison. I rang the bell, he came, and I commenced to give him the introduction by saying, "Mr. Stowell, this is my friend Mr. Garrison, who s to lecture this evening in your house on the subject of slavery." He turned his back immediately upon us, and as he was closing the door, I added, "You will be in to the lecture I suppose." The door closed, and we drove on. Mr. Garrison said to me, "That was a peculiar way to show his Christianity to an infidel." Mr. G. said this because they called him an infidel. But the lecture came off, the Baptist minister being present, and endorsing Mr. Garrison entire.

Truth was mighty about this time, and our Chris

tian abolitionists in Groton had commenced revival meetings, and there was an interest for the salvation of men. A goodly number were inquiring what they should do to be saved. Conviction began to rest heavily upon me, as it did before many times, but I said, "Not now"; yet I felt deeply the need of what I had not. The meetings became more and more interesting. Some were converted, and their experiences told on me as nothing ever did before. The voices of young and old that were heard declaring what the Lord had done for them—the confessions of sins and desire expressed for the prayers of Christians—this increased my conviction. I followed up the meetings, but came home as I went, only more deeply convicted, while a voice seemed to say to me, "Now or never." This startled me, and I could get no rest day or night for a number of days. I tried to see the minister and deacons, but they seemed to keep me off, or did not appreciate my strong convictions of sin and fear of a coming judgment; for I wanted a preparation for that event. The Lord had hold of me, and I felt wretched indeed. I sought pardon. I had had Bible instruction from childhood. I knew that there must be a renewal of my whole being to bring me into the divine favor and the love of God which passeth all understanding.

At length, after calling upon all the helps around me, I looked it over in the light of the Bible, and became convinced that I must have help directly from the Lord. I went to my room, and alone with him I confessed my sins and prayed that he would receive me. I counted the cost, and came to the solemn conclusion that I must make a contract with the Lord and Saviour, and pledge that I would give myself to him in a covenant, binding as long as life should last. This I did. I there gave myself to him, and without any reservation pledged that I would be his for life. Oh, that hour! never to be forgotten! From darkness to light! from the power of satan unto the living God! Now to wait for his Son from heaven. No fear of the judgment now. I was filled with the love of Christ. My load of condemnation was gone. I was as free as the air. My whole being was made to rejoice. My soul and all that was within me was made glad in sins forgiven. It was blessed, yea, twice blessed. I could shout and tell of the preciousness of Christ my Lord, who was all in all to me. All heaven smiled. The sun shone brighter than ever before. Everything looked new, and I felt new. I could say, that whereas I was once blind, now I see. I was a new man. I believed I was converted. I was new at home; new abroad; new at meeting; new everywhere.

This commenced my religious life. Now I could pray as well as talk. From my childhood I had been with good Congregationalists—always with them, contending for their faith, arguing with their opponents and maintaining my position; now when I came to have the faith a living reality, vitalizing my whole being, it was not hard to talk to those who opposed themselves to the truth of God. I could now turn the tables on them and say experimentally: "I know that my Redeemer liveth"; and the blessing came in witnessing of my hope. I found it hard work to keep still. My talent was improved on all proper occasions with blessed results, both with regard to myself and others, as I believed.

CHAPTER V.

United with the Church.

AFTER a time I united with the Congregational Church, and as the Lord seemed to direct went out with others in the neighborhood and vicinity holding meetings, visiting families, beseeching them to run to Christ, the living fountain, and be saved. I always prayed with them. The goodness of the Lord in bringing me into such a glorious light and the freedom of the gospel caused my "cup to run over." So I had to work it out while God worked in me. Revival meetings were the desire uppermost in my mind. Thus I was ever engaged on this line of duty. While at my work in the shoe-shop and in the business, I had many opportunities to talk with radical men who loved the freedom of thought and speech. At this time the subject of temperance, abolition, antimasonry, Christian union, Christian perfection were freely and constantly discussed. This gave me a wide field and access to many who, while they all were interested in one or more of these subjects, had no real interest in their own salvation. I brought this in with the other subjects, and the blessing of the Lord attended my humble efforts. I also engaged in the temperance and antislavery cause, and attended Conventions, at one time going to New York and occupying many places of public interest and importance ; so that I could speak in behalf of the truth and every form of righteousness with a good degree of freedom. It was then said of me, "Boutelle is preaching." I did not call it preaching, but endeavored to keep doing my duty; letting my light shine. I had no hold-back in my wife. She rejoiced in the same Saviour and hope. Thus we made progress together in the divine life. Although poor and working hard to sustain my family, by the help of the Lord we got along wonderfully well, lacking no needed thing. I was in earnest in the religion which I by the grace of God professed, doing all I could to have others come and taste and see if this salvation was not worth having and enjoying. My Christianity took in the non-resistant principle very thoroughly, and I began to see that I was doomed to be among the few. My father and mother were pleased indeed to have me on the Lord's side ; but I was inclined to run too fast for them. While they were exceeding glad that I had been converted, they were fearful that my associations with the leaders in the abolition cause would be greatly against my spiritual life—with such men as Garrison, Thompson, Phillips, May, Douglas, Storrs, Garrett Smith and a host of others pleading for human goods and chattels, sold at auction—that the chains of slavery might be taken off, and the colored *man* have a right to himself, his wife and his children. I was some persecuted, but truth and righteousness urged me on through evil as well as good report, never regretting that I was made of no reputation for my colored brethren and Christ's sake; but counted it all joy.

Being active in my make-up, I had to be stirring, my "new man" leading me to be in love with the work of publishing his name everywhere. In meetings of worship I improved every opportunity to do good. I was out of town, as well as in town, getting up meetings. I went to Townsend, Littleton, and other places and held meetings in school-houses, getting the people together, with good success in awaking a revival interest. It was a great blessing to me, doubly so, because of the salvation of others. I often visited my aged parents, sometimes holding meetings with them, or attending their meeting. Thus I tried to work out my salvation with fear and trembling; my wife and I, one in the same blessed work. I had to be very diligent and economical in order to take care of my family, but my duty in the field of salvation had to be done. My meeting work had to be attended to, if other things suffered a little. I could often go to the meeting, and work two hours after returning home, making my going to rest late at night. Delightful work, this working with God in saving men from death—that they might obtain eternal life, through Jesus Christ our Lord.

I was now in the Congregational church, in good standing. But I was inclined to run faster than the old school brethren thought safe. They were pro-slavery, and exceedingly afraid of the doctrine of holiness and perfection. So we had some stirring times on these subjects. Some of the members had gone so far in advance of the church in advocating their faith in these Bible doctrines, that their excommunication was determined upon. I plead their case. I asked the church to show from the Bible that their faith was anti-scriptural, or to bring forward one text that would show their belief antagonistic to the word of God. This they did not try to do, but they said, we were believing and talking contrary to the creed of the church. They were given three months in which to confess their errors; but if at the end of that time they still held to them, they would no longer be considered members of the church. So they were excommunicated. It was then that I fully began the warfare against the traditions of men, and contending for the faith once delivered to the saints. This kept me at work. I not only took an interest in having men saved from sin, but I was deeply interested in the cause of the slave. I felt that I should do all I could for the abolition of slavery. So I united with others in opposing the terrible evil in a political manner. When the abolitionists undertook to run their men in between the other two parties to defeat them, or have them take our men, I did quite a work in distributing votes and documents throughout the country. But I did not work in this way long before I found my labor futile and all lost; for when you came to the nomination of candidates, your ideal man for the place was suggested, but he must be left off, as he was not available, and the next man be substituted, and he so conservative that the vital principle contended for was lost sight of, and the labor was lost.

This paralyzed my political zeal; so for years I was not seen at the polls. Moral suasion and political action do not work well in conjunction. Political action will have its own way, right or wrong. Moral principle goes in for the right way, and no other. Moral principle rights the wrong; then the right stays put. The political love of country seeks promotion and large salaries. Farther than this it does not often go. There is but little love of making sacrifice without full pay. But all for our country's good (?). Self-denial in political parties is seldom seen; truth and the right are lost sight of. Hence the cursed system of slavery continued until the slavery section of the country rebelled against the government, and attempted to set up another, antagonistic to it, under which they could perpetrate human oppression and slavery. This rebellion against the government opened the eyes of the rest of the nation, and a war began, as great as ever there was. The war ended slavery, and nothing else would have done it. It was a terrible punishment of the whole nation, but God had directed this only way of destroying the power of making chattels of men, women and children.

Long before the war I was a hot abolitionist and reformer. In spite of all opposition I went forward and made my mark. I was a positive man, and every one knew where to put me. Back in the early antislavery times I began to see that the religious world was not in harmony with the Bible; and the more I had to do with these reforms, which were fought against by the great body of the religious denominations, the more evident it became that

Christianity, the world over, was one thing; that Christ was one, his followers were one; "one faith, one Lord, one baptism." The more I thought it over, studying into the subject, the Spirit helping my infirmities, the plainer it appeared to me that we had a standard, the Bible, by which to settle all these questions of reform, and that the opinions of men as such amounted to nothing.

About this time I had affliction in my family. One of my twin babies sickened, and after a while died in my arms. Great was the sorrow to us. This took place July 31, 1838. The baby was fourteen months old. This left us with two children. As a family we were getting along as well as we could. The times were hard. There was great depression in business, especially the shoe business, in which I was engaged in company with Deacon Cragin. We stopped our business, partly from necessity, as there was a bankruptcy of the market for our goods. But nevertheless, bread and water came. I retained my homestead for the good and comfort of my family and relatives. We were happy in our domestic relations, and at peace with our neighbors. So as we were on good terms with all around us, far and near, all went well, while we grew in grace and the knowledge of God through his blessed word. My conversion, as I have said, made me a new man in Christ. This harmonized all my reform principles, and made me a better antislavery man than before. In these reforms I had nothing to take back. They added strength and vigor to my youthful manhood. My house was the home of all the stigmatized reformers and free religionists. I was well known among them as the friend of freedom, life and liberty; and reckoned among those who "turn the world upside down." I seemed to belong to this class without any effort of my own. I could not keep out of it. I was always diligent and ready to do with my might what I could, and with the ability which God had given me.

I often visited my father and mother in these years, and they were always delighted in seeing me and my family. Calvin, my twin brother lived in the same town with father and mother, but probably I visited them as often as he, notwithstanding I lived so much farther away. I was rather a favorite of my mother. I resembled her in looks and ways, while Calvin was more like father. There was a marked difference in our organizations, and the contrast grew no less as we grew older.

As I have said, on account of the great depression in business at this time (1837-8) we had to close up; and a little later we dissolved and settled, I coming out second best. This brought some anxiety relative to the future; but my trust was in the Lord, and I did the very best I could. I still visited my venerable parents often, looking after their interests; for while I had all my own affairs to attend to, it was my delight to look after the welfare of others. This kept me on a stir; home duties to perform, and going into "the regions beyond." Oh, how I loved it! Thus time went rapidly on, and at home and abroad I was cheerful and happy.

CHAPTER VI.

A Strange Sound—New Subject.

ABOUT this time a strange sound came on the air: "The world is coming to an end! Christ is coming to judgment!" It came nearer and caused much thinking and talk, which daily grew upon us. Finally we heard that a Vermont farmer was preaching it and was coming to Lowell. This caused a stir among us, and the question was: What shall we in Groton do to hear this new doctrine? We concluded that if the Congregational meeting-house could be had for a lecture, we would send and invite the man who was preaching this new doctrine to come and speak to us. I was to see the pastor of the church and get his consent to the use of the house. I did so, and obtained the house for one lecture. So we sent for Mr. Miller, and received a reply that he would come, he setting the time. This commenced a new era in my history.

While I had been active through all my religious life; had been full of excitement with little abatement, now there was a mighty wakeing up. Mr. Miller came according to appointment. He took the second chapter of Daniel for his subject. The house was full, and all were earnest hearers, ready to criticise every thing that was said. The exposition of each verse carried conviction, and a most anxious hearing was manifest. None could evade his conclusions. The interest was so great that many said, "We want to hear further on this subject." As we could not have the meeting-house for any more lectures, we went to a good hall near by and heard for a week the argument for the Lord's soon coming. And it took hold of us as nothing ever did before. A religious interest was at once awakened, and the people mightily aroused. A searching of the Bible, from the beginning to the end, was witnessed, and a deep anxiety to know how Mr. Miller understood each part, and what he had to say. But there was a deeper inquiry: "What shall I do to be saved?" It seemed at first as though all were coming into the belief of the Lord's soon appearing. But presently there was opposition seen. The church and clergy came out against the preaching of the doctrine, and a conflict began. But there was so much of the Spirit and power of God with this message, that those who had any vital salvation in them could not help believeing it; and the first you knew you would be saying "Amen," the word penetrating you through and through.

I remember well, after an evening lecture by Mr. Miller on some part of the prophecy of Daniel, coming home with my wife, who digested and felt the force of the solemn application he made of his subject, she said, reviewing some part of his subject, "Don't you believe that, husband?" I said "Wife, it is Bible, but I hardly think I believe it." She replied, earnestly, "Well, if it is Bible, why don't you believe it?" I had looked it over solemnly, and so I said, "When I believe it you will know it, for I shall have to leave you and run with the message." I thought within myself, there is salvation in it, and I shall have to go.

The tide of Millerism, as they called it, rose higher and higher, until, like the rushing of many waters, it swept over the land. There seemed to be little else talked of. It was the theme of ministers, deacons, class-leaders and praying-bands, some opposing, but the most impressed deeply with the subject. The spiritual in the churches fell in with it joyfully, saying, "This is the truth! Glory! Hallelujah!" Such was the effect of believing that message that men who loved the world and were covetous, became benevolent, and gave to the cause of Christ and the poor. Christ was a new Saviour, the Bible a new book; so they felt. The word of God seemed to electrify all who believed this doctrine of Christ's soon coming. They saw a harmony in it, and an import they had never seen before. The work of redemption culminating at the coming of Jesus Christ to judgment was clearly seen.

Meetings where we lived were soon daily things. I had become fully converted to the doctrine of Adventism, and could tell, in my way, the pleasing story. My honored parents had wanted a son in the ministry. But I had not been prepared in their way. The Lord wanted me prepared in his way; so I was brought along by him. He had raised me up from sickness and death's door when all hope of life had vanished. I was preserved, not knowing for what purpose. He brought me out of darkness into his marvelous light, and from sin and satan unto himself. Now he had shown me what his word taught, filled me with his Spirit, and should I not preach, preach the great salvation, and the coming of his Son to finish it? So I said to my wife, "This message is everything, and I am on the wing to proclaim it. The Lord is soon coming; I am filled with the Spirit, and must preach the preaching that he bids me." I heard the voice, and I said,

"Lord, here am I." I had to leave house, land, wife and children, and bear a mighty reproach at the hands of my best Christian brethren, as I then thought them to be, and step forth, trusting in Him who "called me to glory and virtue." I had no obstacles in the way at home. My wife drank the same cup of salvation, and called on the same Lord. I had no sooner started out than doors were opened on every hand, and it was only to step right along. We had nothing to do with Mission Societies then. It was simply, What will please the Lord? He said to me, "This message must be delivered, will you go?" I said, "Yea, Lord," and started. Heaven called, I could not but obey. The impulse by the Spirit of God, and this God-honored message gave great boldness. There was no waiting for an outfit; the belief that the Lord was at the doors made every one ready to tell the story of his coming. The Spirit of the Lord working mightily on men's minds, caused them to go to the Bible to learn its teachings relative to Jesus' soon appearing. To many it was, "Go preach." To others it was, "Go pray and exhort." All felt the responsibility of the call, and without fear of consequences went out into unknown fields to give the alarm and help save the perishing.

Here was a conflict with the wisdom of the world

which never harmonizes with the wisdom of God. But the voice came, "Follow thou me"; then all was still within, and peace that passeth all understanding flowed into the heart. So without money or scrip we accepted the position and started out in the proclamation of this message, leaving all to spread it abroad. I had bitter opposition from my old brethren, as I have said; but a sweet fellowship with my new brethren, all lovers of Jesus and his soon appearing. I had come into an affinity with a people, that what they had they did not call their own. It was, "Behold, he cometh," and this was to be sounded everywhere. It was wonderful how rapidly it spread. It went like fire over a prairie. Soon the towns and cities called for meetings and light on the subject of the coming King. Calls in every direction were heard: "Come over and tell us this new thing." Without any system of labor marked out, you stand on the watch-tower, and when the call comes, the only thing to inquire is, is it from the Lord? This was determined by prayer and fasting, and having found that you should go, then you must. Sublime spectacle, the army of the Lord's preachers moving hither and thither to their fields of labor in one accord, declaring the same heaven-sent message. The spiritual minded disciples of Jesus would fall in love with it at once. All were moved as never before. Sinners were alarmed and came to the fountain of life: Christ the way, the truth and the life.

CHAPTER VII.

Leaving Home to Give the Message.

IN that mighty movement I began my ministry in earnest. I had so many calls and entreaties to come, that I could not stop to consult ease or comfort, or ask what people might think. They scolded and scoffed, but I was doing my specific work. I was soon found in Nashua, Ashburnham and Lowell, at meetings, and these opened other doors; and if I could have been divided into four parts, all could have been put in motion by the calls which came from all directions. The hand of God was as visible as if he had stood by my side. The reminiscence of those golden times comes with a rush into my mind, and I look back over my pilgrimage then with wonder at the grace that was shown me. My first winter's labor was mostly in Vermont. I had then obtained a degree of boldness surprising to myself. I had a call to Grafton, Vt., to assist in an Advent meeting to be held there. I knew no one there except a friend who had seen me in Massachusetts. He being in Grafton, sent for me to come and attend some meetings there, giving me the time when they were to be held. I took the matter to the Lord in prayer, and the answer came that I should go. Wife inquired if I were going. I said, "Yes." She then asked how I was to get there. I replied, "By the promises of God." I at once wrote that I would come. I then made preparations for leaving my family. I did my best to leave them in comfortable circumstances, feeling assured that the Lord would be with them.

When the time came to begin the journey, I got the offer of a ride on the way of seven miles. On leaving, my little boy clung to me until my heart was almost melted. I gave him my last penny but one, and told him to be a good boy. I bade good-bye to all, and started. Rode that seven miles to my first stopping-place, where there was to be an evening meeting. I had a good time using my gift. They inquired where I was bound. I told them. They thought it a long journey, and made inquiries in regard to my means of getting through. I told them I had one penny and the promise of God. Brother Heath said, "You then will get there." Brother R. asked what time I would like to leave in the morning. I said as soon as seven o'clock. At 7 A. M. this brother drove up to the door in his sleigh, and took me in; and so I was joyfully on my way. He was intending to carry me as far as he could and return the same day. We had gone but a short distance, when I incidentally said, that it would be a convenient thing to have a team in going out to preach this message. He immediately pulled up upon the reins and stopped, saying, "Why not take this team and move right along on your journey?" I hesitated, but said, "Brother, you need this horse more than I do." He said, "No, I would rather you would take it than not, for my hay is short." After talking the matter over, I accepted his offer. He then gave me money for feeding the horse on the journey, and left me, going back on foot to his home. "Thus far the Lord had led me on."

I now made my best way to Grafton, Vt. Came into the town at noon, on Sunday, expecting to find an Advent meeting in session. I called at the hotel and inquired if there was such a meeting. They said, none that they knew of. After a time, not knowing what next to do, I heard the church bell ring, and saw the people going thither. I went into the house with them and took a seat near the stove. It was a Baptist Church. A sermon was preached, to which I listened attentively, wondering why I was there. At the close of the sermon the minister told the congregation that he would be absent two weeks, but he had supplied the desk, and that they must keep up the interest while he was away. Just then a man stepped up to the desk and handed the minister a paper, which he read. It was something like this: "There will be a lecture to-morrow evening in the Center School-house, on the 'Coming of the Lord,' by a Mr. Boutelle from the East." That, being read, the congregation were dismissed. I then asked the man who sat near me to introduce me to the gentleman who handed the notice to the minister, saying to him that I was the one referred to in the notice. He introduced me as I requested, and I found the man to be Bro. Gibson, a member of the Baptist Church. He was the father of Eld. O. D. Gibson, who afterward was an earnest Advent preacher in the West; and who died there a few years since. Bro. G. took me to his home, and bade me welcome. Monday evening came, and I went with Bro. G. to the school-house, which was already crowded with people of all ages, and of course all strangers to me. But the message must be delivered. I commenced by singing one of our inspired Advent hymns. All eyes were upon me, and all ears open. After prayer, in which the Holy Spirit helped me, and again singing, I told them my errand among them. It was to give the evidences of the coming of the Lord Jesus Christ, which was good news to every one who loved him, and a reason why all who did not love him should at once come and be saved, and ready for his appearing. I added that if a place could be found for meetings, I would stay and endeavor to prove from the Bible that Christ was near, even at the doors. I then gave them an introductory talk on the twenty-fourth of Matthew. Every standing place was occupied, and the interest ran high. All listened as never before, it seemed to me. The infidels of the place were out to see and hear.

After I was through, the question of future meetings was talked upon. It did not take long to settle it, however. Bro. Gibson being a member of the Baptist Church there, felt that the meetings should be held in the meeting-house; but the minister was away and the committee did not like to assume the responsibility of opening the house; so there was a perplexity. It was finally decided that we go into the house, and if we were turned out, then we would quietly leave and seek another place. So we appointed a meeting the next day at half past nine, A. M., inviting all, and requesting that all come to pray for the blessing of God. We also appointed a meeting at 10.30, when we would give them a lecture on the second chapter of Daniel. We also appointed a meeting at 2 o'clock, and another at 7, when we would preach on the signs of our Lord's coming; and that this would be the order of exercises for each day of the week. This went out, and was the subject of conversation in all the region around. The morning came, but with a snow storm during the night, which made it look a little dubious. But it soon cleared away, and before our meeting hour, the people with a long team of oxen and a sled broke out the roads, and made a good path right to the meeting-house door, so that at our first meeting a goodly number were present, and took hold with us. At 10.30 we had a good congregation, which was increased at the afternoon and evening meetings, and through the week with great interest.

After preaching the first evening, a deep feeling was manifested. Conviction rested upon the people mightily, and the cry was soon heard, "What shall I do to be saved?" The house was full. I said, in closing, "We are not here to make Baptists, Methodists, Congregationalists or any other sect, but to make Christians; and all of you that desire to be Christ's and ready for his coming, please come forward for prayers, and go with us to the kingdom of God." At once it seemed as if the whole congregation were on their feet. All seats in the house seemed to be anxious seats. All we could do was to request them to yield themselves to Christ where they were; and in a closing prayer we committed them to the Lord. It was a glorious sight and a heavenly season; one never to be forgotten by me. We now had converts daily, and to God we gave all the glory. Every day added to the interest.

We remained there ten days. Many came into the faith. Two young men became so strong in the faith that they went to preaching it, and the region around was filled with the sound: "Behold, he cometh." We left a large number of converts there.

While there we were urged to come to Londonderry, Vt., with a promise of the Baptist house, in which to preach. The time was set for the meetings to begin, which was the next Saturday evening. Accordingly Bro. Gibson hitched up his span and took in a sleigh load for Londonderry. When we got into the town we began to give notice of the meeting that evening at the Baptist Church. We went on in good cheer doing this until we arrived at our stopping-place. Our friend there gave us a hearty welcome, but informed us that the meeting-house could not be opened, as the key was lost! Thus we were left in a sad dilemma. But close by stood the Congregational meeting-house. It was not very showy, and looked as though it might welcome the coming of the Lord. We were now at a loss to know what to do. A notice had gone out of a meeting that evening, and no door was open for it. Finally our friend said, that we would go to the Center School-house. There was to be a school-meeting there that evening, but he thought they might give up their meeting for us. So we went there, and stated our case. The keeper of the village hotel being present, said, "Go tell my hostler to fire and light my hall as soon as possible, and you invite the people there." So after much perseverance and delay, the people, sixty or seventy, were got into the hall. We hardly knew where to begin, but this text came to mind, 1 Thess. 5: 21, "Prove all things." After looking to the Lord in prayer, I read my text, and from it told my hearers, that I was not there for their money, nor to build up any party in religion, but was there to prove to them by the Bible that the Lord Jesus Christ was soon coming, when there would be a resurrection of the dead and the judgment. I said to them that if I did not prove it by the Bible, I did not want any one to believe it; but if I did prove it, I wanted all to believe it and get ready for the coming day. This with some practical lessons, and then I said, if a place for meetings could be obtained, I would stay eight or ten days and speak to the people. After I sat down, a man arose and said, "My friends, I have been hearing what this stranger has said to us with a great deal of interest, and as he has told us that he shall prove by the Bible what he wants us to believe, and that he has not come to build up sects, but to have us believe the simple word of God, his claim upon our hearing seems reasonable. I endorse what he has said here to-night, and if he will accept the use of our church, it is ready for him." I then inquired what church it was. He said it was the Congregational, and that he was the pastor. We accepted his offer thankfully, and gave notice, that by his permission we would commence a series of meetings there the next day (Sunday), to continue daily through the week. At 9.30 A. M., there would be a prayer meeting, at which we wanted to see all that loved to pray. That at 10.30 we would speak on the signs of the Lord's coming. At 2 P. M. a short prayer meeting, followed by preaching. At 7.30 preaching. That this would be the program through the week. The minister took me home with him; so the Lord did direct and provide.

We opened our meeting Sunday morning according to appointment. The house was soon filled with an interested congregation. The Baptist people, with the key of their house lost, opened their house that morning; but as none of the church except the minister and the two deacons went into it, it was locked again and they came over to our meeting.

They wanted us to come to their house, but we continued in the Congregational house for ten days or more, witnessing the most powerful work of salvation we had then seen. The interest increased, the converts were multiplied, and the region for miles around was stirred as never before. The near coming of the Lord was the great theme. Soon after the meetings commenced we held inquiry meetings in the school-house, while the prayer meetings were going on in the meeting-house. The people all flocked to our meetings. Three Methodist ministers from other towns came daily to our meetings. Such a time of confessing, and the forgiving of one another I never saw. Such a returning to the Lord by wandering professors of religion; and the inquiry, "What shall I do to be saved"—this was soul-reviving. Surely God by his Spirit was in the midst of the people. We could but pray, preach and shout while the angels in heaven were rejoicing.

After remaining there longer than I supposed I should when the work began, I left, but with reluctance; for it was delightfully blessed to see the Lord work as he did in the conversion of perishing men, making them ready for his expected kingdom. I had a good fellow-worker with me in these meetings.

The singing was in the Spirit and with the understanding also. Then we sang:

> "We are a band of brethren dear;
> I will be in this band, Hallelujah.
> Our Leader tells us not to fear;
> I will be in this band, Hallelujah.
> I will be in this band, Hallelujah,
> In the Second Advent band, Hallelujah."

We were not ashamed then to sing this and other like hymns. They were full of meaning then. This was Adventism in its early days, when the Lord was with us by the Spirit, convicting and converting scores and hundreds wherever the soon coming of the Lord was proclaimed.

CHAPTER VIII.

Returning Home—Incidents

AFTER lecturing in some other places I returned home to look after my family, from whom I had heard every week while gone. Here I want to put in a short golden brief to show how the Lord had his eye upon his cause and his people; how he took care of both, being a present help in time of need. I have told the reader how I started out on this trip with a penny and the promise of God. I left home on Thursday morning. On the Sunday morning after, my door-bell rang. My wife went to the door, and who should be there but old Bro. Wood from Dunstable, with his wife and daughter. Bro. W. was an acquaintance of mine, a Congregationalist. He had begun to feel that the Lord was soon coming, and he was not ready, and had come nine miles to be prayed for, and to see into the blessed doctrine. My wife told him that I had gone to Vermont, but they must come in, and they would have a meeting, which was soon collected. Bro. Wood and family were made the special subjects of prayer, and for the Divine favor. A great blessing was received; the season long remembered. On returning home, Bro. Wood and wife left their daughter in my family, and he was so interested in their behalf that he visited them two and three times a week during my absence, seeing them well cared for, and that they lacked no good thing. While looking after my folks, he learned that I had gone preaching the Lord's coming, and left word that when I returned I must come and see him.

After my return, I accordingly with my wife went and made Bro. Wood a visit. By his desire I rehearsed how the Lord had dealt with me, and glorified himself in the proclamation of the great message, stirring the people and converting many. He was greatly interested in the account, while his faith was strengthened in the word of God. When I was ready to leave, he presented me with forty dollars, which he understood I owed one of my neighbors. This I gratefully accepted as from the Lord. On reaching home, I went and paid the man I owed. This stopped the mouths of all scoffers, charging me with wrong-doing. Thus you see the Lord cared both for my family and myself. Oh, how safe it is to trust in the mighty God! "Go ye into my vineyard, and whatsoever is right I will give you," was verified to me. The new pentecostal times had come. Those who had the Spirit poured out upon them then, did not call what they had their own. This same good Bro. W. was ready for every good word and work, and he did a great deal for the cause.

This was my first long tour in the itinerancy; after which I visited many places. This angel's message was a flying one. No man that had it could keep still. Campmeetings were held; Conferences attended. I visited these in Massachusetts, Connecticut, and New Hampshire. Bro. Miller was present in many of them. The interest increased everywhere. New England was filled with what was called by way of reproach, "Millerism." This was Adventism, and will be called so until Jesus comes. After this I was never out of work. The calls were many. I visited Westmoreland, N. H. I went and held meetings with Elder T. M. Preble with good success. The Lord gave great freedom in the preaching the "glad tidings" of his coming. We were bold, and often invited the congregation to ask any question relative to the subject under consideration, which was as often done, we never failing to answer all questions that were asked to the apparent satisfaction of the inquirer, if not to our own. The word of the Lord triumphed gloriously. The echo of the word spoken would come from the hills: "Behold, he cometh with clouds; and every eye shall see him." The air seemed to be full of the sound. 1843 was a memorable epoch. We could not keep from speaking. The church had to speak, or the word of God be broken. We were workers with God, and God spoke through us with an unmistakable voice. The hearers of this voice were obeyers and doers. They were one in Christ, one in faith, marching on in the light of prophecy, aided by the Holy Spirit. Beautiful sight for the angels to look upon; they seeming to say: "Run and tell the good news."

After this my time was all occupied in preaching in different States, at Campmeetings, Conferences and other meetings. As time rolled on and the year 1843 passed (in which we all looked for the Lord), the interest kept up and it was with deep solicitude that we entered 1844. Signs were still showing that we were near the great event. The great landmark of 1780 was remembered, with the later ones, and these with the "great tribulation" held us fast. Other fulfillments of prophecy hurried us on with heads uplifted, believing that our redemption was nigh.

I went to Portland, Maine. Visited Deacon Pearson. Went with him to the hall there where the

Adventists were holding large meetings. Went and held meetings also in Concord, N. H., Worcester, Springfield, Chicopee, Hartford, Bristol, Conn., and many other places, and saw the wonderful work of the Lord, in causing men to "renounce the hidden things of dishonesty," and come to Christ by a manifestation of the truth; thus showing that they had been regenerated. Adventists were bold then. They worked with a will; were hated and persecuted; for the last-day scoffers had come, saying, "Where is the promise of his coming?" Many interesting incidents occurred in this rush for the kingdom, when the violent were taking it by force. Some of these incidents are worth remembering and relating, showing the Lord's hand in the work. In my itinerating I found a young man by the name of James Hemenway, in a spindle factory in Concord. He and his wife fell in love with Jesus' soon coming, and had meetings at their house. He soon became uneasy in his factory work, and left it to blow the trumpet of alarm, and arouse the people to prepare for the judgment. We helped him in this what we could. We went together, he with me to improve his gift in the meetings. He rapidly improved in speaking. He was with me at one of my appointments at a certain place in Massachusetts. After a time I went there alone. While the people were gathering in the house, I heard one man ask another if they had preaching the Sunday preceding. The reply was, "Yes; Boutelle's apprentice preached to us, and he beat the old man out and out." Well, I heard that with great joy; and I thought how quickly the Lord can raise up some men to do a greater work than others. Then I was glad that I had helped the young man into the field, and that he could preach so much better than myself. I prayed for an increase of faith, love, humility, strength and ability to preach this all-important message. Bro. H. is in the work, and the work is in him, thought I. The vineyard is the world, and the promise is, "Lo, I am with you always." The "little book" had been eaten, and the sweet message of the flying angel had been heard. The winds of heaven had taken it all over the world in spite of all opposition. It was a sublime spectacle to see the trumpeters fall in, sounding, "Behold, he cometh!" It was like pentecost to see two families take from the same barrel, without either saying, "This is mine." Holiness, justification, sanctification came easy then, with rejoicing such as is not now manifested. This was our early experience. The Lord be praised. Amen.

CHAPTER IX.

Great Interest in the Coming of Christ.

AS we entered upon the year 1844, the interest, instead of decreasing, kept up; and during the summer the number of Campmeetings, Grovemeetings and Conferences increased, and the workers in the Lord's vineyard had all that they could do.

In the early part of the summer our attention was directed to the fall as the time for the Lord to come, according to the types in the Old Testament, which began to be studied and preached. By July there was such a concentration of thought among the strong ones on time, that it was called "the midnight cry." Thus a new impetus was created, and the work of holding meetings and preaching was increased. As we fell, one after another, into the current belief that the fall would witness the coming of our Lord, it became in faith a certainty—we believed it with our whole souls. Thus the cry, "Behold, the bridegroom cometh!" was, by the "time argument," made to end in the fall of 1844, Jewish time, tenth day of the seventh month, supposed to be Oct. 20, 21, or 22. This brought us to a definite time, and in coming up to it, the works of Adventists demonstrated their faith and honesty, not to be questioned. As they moved on with the point of time before them, all grew more enthusiastic. Crops were left unharvested, their owners expecting never to want what they had raised. Men paid up their debts. Many sold their property to help others to pay their debts, who could not have done it themselves. Beef cattle were slaughtered and distributed among the poor. At no time since "the day of pentecost was fully come" had there been the like—a day when that pentecost was so completely duplicated as in 1844, when Adventism prevailed and reigned.

There was a great stir and talk, in many places, about putting the Millerites under guardianship. But this did not cause any to go back on their faith. They were firm and held fast, believing they should speak and act. Thus they were known by their fruits. There was some fanaticism, but the body of Adventists were sober, honest, a holy people, with strong faith and ready to meet their Lord—to see the King in his beauty. As the time to which all looked drew near, the Bible was studied even more, and a fuller consecration made. There was a harmony that made us a unit at this time, and the representatives of Adventism and the flock were all one.

CHAPTER X.

The Great Disappointment.

THE *Advent Herald*, the *Midnight Cry*, and other Advent papers, periodicals, pamphlets, tracts, leaflets, voicing the coming glory, were scattered broadcast and everywhere, like autumn leaves in the forest. Every house was visited by them. They were angels of mercy sent in love for the salvation of men. Everything now began to converge to a point. October was the closing time of probation! the judgment and rewards! A mighty effort through the Spirit and the word preached was made to bring sinners to repentance, and to have the wandering return. All were awake to this great end—salvation. The tenth day of the seventh month drew nigh. With joy all the ready ones anticipated the day. Solemn, however, were the last gatherings. Those of a family who were ready to meet the Lord, expecting an eternal separation from those who were not ready. Husbands and wives, parents and children, brothers and sisters separated, and that forever! The leading preachers of Adventism had all endorsed the tenth day of the seventh month as the time when the Lord should be expected. On Oct. 6, Mr. Miller accepted the argument as true, and wrote an endorsement of it.

Geo. Storrs, Sept. 24, 1844, in the *Bible Examiner* said, "I take my pen with feelings such as I never had before. Beyond a doubt in my mind the tenth day of the seventh month will witness the revelation of our Lord Jesus Christ from heaven."

The *Voice of Truth*, of Oct. 2, stated that Elders Marsh, Galusha, Peavy and others had endorsed it.

In closing the *Advent Herald* office on the 16th of October, an immense edition of that paper was issued for free distribution in all parts of the land. This was considered the last edition ever to be published.

We now give an extract from Bro. S. Bliss. He wrote, "The time immediately preceding the 22nd of October was one of great calmness of mind and pleasurable expectation on the part of those who regarded the point of time with interest. There was a nearness of approach to God, and a sacredness of communion with him, to which those who experienced it will ever recur with pleasure. During the last ten days secular business was, for the most part, suspended, and those who looked for the advent gave themselves to the work of preparation for the event as they would for death, were they on a bed of sickness, expecting soon to close their eyes on earthly scenes forever."—*History of the Second Advent Message.*

These quotations harmonize with what I knew to be at the time. Such a concentration of thought; such a oneness of faith was never before witnessed; certainly not in modern times. All that did speak spoke the same things. Solemn, yet joyful. Jesus coming! we to meet him! Meetings everywhere were being held. Confessions made, wrongs righted; sinners inquiring what they should do to be saved. Those who were not with us were mightily effected. Some were exceedingly frightened with awful forebodings.

But the 22nd of October passed, making unspeakably sad the faithful and longing ones; but causing the unbelieving and wicked to rejoice. All was still. No *Advent Herald;* no meetings as formerly. Every one felt lonely, with hardly a desire to speak to any one. Still in the cold world! No deliverance—the Lord not come! No words can express the feelings of disappointment of a true Adventist then. Those only who experienced it can enter into the subject as it was. It was a humiliating thing, and we all felt it alike. All were silent, save to inquire, "Where are we?" and "What next?" All were housed and searching their Bibles to learn what to do. In some few places they soon began to come together to watch for some development of light, relative to our disappointment.

Not quite content with being housed, after such stirring times, I went to Boston. Found the *Advent Herald* office closed, and all still. I next went to New Bedford. Found the brethren in a confused state. Had a few meetings; comforted those who came as best I could, telling them to hold fast, for I believed there would be a good come out of this matter. Returning from New Bedford to Boston, I found the office of our *Herald* open, and Bro. Bliss there. He said he had hardly been from his house since the time passed. He inquired if there were any meetings being held. I told him there was to be one in the city that evening, and that in other places they were coming together to comfort one another. Some fanaticism was seen, but the many were sober watchers for their Lord.

I learned of a company that had come together to stay until the Lord came. I felt like visiting them. Accordingly I took a carriage ride to the place. I found about seventy believers in a large house, living there and having meetings daily. They had put all their money in a milk-pan, and when they paid for anything they took the money from the pan. All was common stock. We held a meeting with them and advised them as best we could to keep the faith and separate, and see to their individual interests, and those of their families, which advice they kindly took, and very soon separated, going each to his and her calling.

After a time in looking over the way the Lord had led us, and bearing the reproach in consequence of our failure, we found there was to be a disappointment in the fulfillment of the parable. The words of Jesus were, "While the bridegroom tarried, they all slumbered and slept." From the first of our experience as Adventists, we believed we were fulfilling the parable by going forth to meet the Lord in our faith and preaching of his coming, but we did not see that the Bridegroom—the Lord—would not come when we expected him. But it was not long after our disappointment before the light began to break in upon us, and we saw there was to be a waiting time, a midnight before the Lord would come. Turning to Rev., tenth chapter, we saw that after the "little book" was eaten, and sweet in the mouth, there was a bitterness to be experienced. Our disappointment was bitter, and it was by eating the word of God, or the little book. Since that time a new inspiration has been given us, and we have done even more than we did before our disappointment; for the little book was to "prophesy again before many peoples, and nations, and tongues, and kings." Thus the word of God is fulfilled by us, and we can still repeat:

> In eighteen hundred forty-four,
> We thought the curse would be no more.
> The things of earth we left behind,
> To meet the Saviour of mankind.
> With many we took the parting hand,
> Till meeting in the better land.
> The day passed by—no tongue can tell
> The gloom that on the faithful fell.
> Then what it meant they hardly knew,
> But to their Lord they quickly flew.
> They searched the Word, and not in vain,
> For comfort there they did obtain.
> They found "the bridge" they had passed o'er;
> Then they rejoiced and grieved no more.
> Their faith was firm in that blest Book,
> And still for Jesus they did look.

CHAPTER XI.

Resuming the Work with Good Courage.

AND now a new era was begun. These divine utterances were heard with such distinctness that it was easy to believe them; and with a zeal equal to our former one, we took hold of the work now given us to do. We found that the truth was not to be all learned at once. Thus we came into the tarrying time. This helped us to bear our disappointment, and put our feet on solid land. Prophecy again rang in our ears, and we were now on the wing again, and the world found Millerism, which they buried, still alive. So while the Bridegroom tarried, meat in due season was to be given. With the assurance of light and divine help we quickened our pace in our itinerating, and soon found the whole body was breathing more freely. We as a people righted up, and the sound of rejoicing was heard. The scattered Advent body was gathered again, and commenced anew their work of love.

In Jan. 1845, the *Advent Herald* appeared again in the field, acknowledging our disappointment, but urging the necessity of keeping the signs of the Lord's soon coming before the people. Thus encouraged, our meetings, Conferences and Campmeetings were resumed with the former interest, while the way opened wonderfully before us for missionary work, scattering the light of the gospel in all directions. We now had calls as many as we could attend to.

My first visit to Maine was going to the Lincolnville Campmeeting. There was a large attendance of the brethren in that State. Here I became acquainted with Bro. Israel Damman and other preaching brethren. We had a very interesting meeting of days, in which the great message was still presented to the people. Some were converted, others reclaimed. The people were greatly stirred up in all that region, many falling in love with the coming of the Lord. Here I became acquainted with many devoted Adventists on the Penobscot River, whom I subsequently visited and labored among, attending Campmeetings at Corinna, Orrington, Brewer and China. Attended Conferences in many places, and preached in towns here and there. I visited old sainted Bro. Chamberlain and preached in his meeting-house in Corinna. He was a singular man, but a man of God. He belonged to the Christian denomination. I went on preaching tours in Maine with Elders Ross, Berrick, Hemenway, Brewer and Goodrich, and saw the gospel of the kingdom received by hundreds, under the direction of the great Captain of our salvation. The sweet memory of persons and places in Penobscot County stays by me. Our brethren at the East were honest-hearted, outspoken, and never took hold of anything to do it at the halves. None could make a mistake in determining which side they were on.

After this I attended a Campmeeting at Newington, Conn. Here was my first acquaintance with Bro. S. G. Mathewson and wife. Here we had a stirring time. King Hastings, Hiram Munger and many other leading brethren were present. The scoffers came to this meeting in force, causing much trouble. Among the things which they did was the throwing showers of apples at King Hastings while he was preaching. But in spite of all opposition the gospel of the kingdom was preached, and was there received by a goodly number. The truth still had a place in the land, and the work went on. The Lord gave us there a demonstration of his power in an unmistakable manner. Divine healing was manifested in the recovery of the sick. Through all our history, as a people, while the angels of God have guarded and protected us, they have witnessed the power of the Almighty in healing many of his humble children of their maladies; while they too have been kept rejoicing over repenting sinners. Blessed be the Lord.

In my mission work I frequently visited Connecticut. I preached in Hartford, New Britain, Bristol, Northfield, Plymouth, Yalesville, Meriden, Wallingford, Winsted, and many other places. In all these I found brethren, houses, homes and places for meetings, where the gospel of the Lord's coming was listened to and rejoiced in. Here we found Col. Hawkins, Judge Tyler, and a host of other intelligent men who were ready to welcome the watchman, and inquire, "What of the night?" The recollection of those times is sweet, for in them the Lord worked marvelously.

There is an incident which happened in Connecticut, which I will here relate. I stopped with a Bro. M. who was a well-to-do farmer. He with a span of colts and a large carriage carried me from place to place with a full load of meeting-goers. On the way, generally, there was singing in the carriage as we rode on. Our people in those days were so vitalized by the Spirit of God that they could sing at all times, and under all circumstances. After we all had sung a certain hymn, I happened to say that one of those horses would make a fine missionary horse, with which to spread the glad tidings of the kingdom at hand. No answer was made to my remark. The singing went on until we got to our stopping-place. After three or more weeks of meetings in this region, Bro. M. took me out to Hartford, on my way home. After a few weeks, while at home in Groton, I received a letter from Bro. M., which read:

"My Bro. Boutelle:—I have a confession to make. That horse which you said would make a good mission horse, I felt I ought to give you, but I did not want to break the span. One day as usual I let my horses, cattle and sheep out to water. They all returned except this horse. I waited for him to come up to the barn, but as he did not come, I went to find him. I found him with his leg broken, and so had to kill him. This was because I did not do as the Lord made known my duty to do. I confess my wrong, praying the Lord to forgive me, and that you will also."

After a time I visited that region again. Found Bro. M., still interested in the things of the kingdom, and helping on the servants of Christ. When I had again ended my work there, and was about to return home, he said he would see me to Hartford, which he did. In Hartford I went to stay with Elder Joseph Turner. Bro. M. went to another place. On leaving me for the night he said, "Shall I not see you in the morning?" I said to him, "I am going to leave quite early." He replied, "I would like to see you." I said, "Where shall I see you?" Bro. M. said, "Meet me at 8 o'clock on Main Street, opposite of Dr. Bushnell's Church." I slept and took breakfast, and at 8 A. M. stepped out upon Main Street, where Bro. M. directed me to meet him. Soon he came up to me, leading a horse, and said, "There, that's for your mission work." All I could say was, "How can I get him along?" He said, "Come with me." I followed him to a stable. He hitched him into a second-hand buggy, saying, "All is yours." Thanking him and the Lord with all my heart I drove off toward home with feelings I cannot describe. This shows how God can work by his Spirit on the minds of his children. Only live near him and you will learn what he wants you to do; and to obey is to have his blessing.

I rode on home praising the Lord for his *wonderful* goodness to me. I could now get along with less money, and visit the poor. We preachers then had no stipulated salaries. What the Lord gave us we were thankful for. If we had reproach, stoning and hardships, they were for Christ's sake; and with the good things of the kingdom besides, we could well be content.

CHAPTER XII.

Still Pressing on in the Work.

AFTER itinerating near home, I started with my horse and carriage on a trip to Maine. Leaving wife and children, as I was wont to do, and taking a Bro. Haskins with me, we drove on, holding meetings on the way wherever we stopped, having blessed good times in "prophesying again" the coming of the Lord, and assuring the people that we were right, and in the "little while" to wait.

We called at Concord, N. H. Found the way open for meetings, and were heartily welcomed with our message. Here we found Bro. Hook, the Brn. Ford, Nevins, Webster and a live company of Adventists. Stopped awhile with them, forming a fellowship that will last as long as this life continues, and renewed in the life to come. From Concord we went to Eaton, making calls on the way. Found some of like precious faith in all the places we passed through. Not keeping a diary, many incidents are forgotten. We would go into places where the district school was in session, and obtaining the schoolhouse for meetings, get the teacher to give out the appointment in the school, when the scholars would carry it to their parents and the neighbors. Generally the house would be filled with eager listeners. This trip to Maine was productive of great good to many.

We remember going into the towns of Sweden and Norway especially. Bro. Haskins having a sister residing in the town of Woodstock, we went there and gave the people the word of the Lord. He made his home with his sister, and we did the same. We remained in this place many days. The Universalist meeting-house was opened for us, and here we delivered our message, the people coming out to hear in good numbers. While here I attended a Grovemeeting. Preached on the twenty-fourth of Mattthew. Gave the people the signs of the Lord's coming. It was a mixed meeting of Adventists and others. Some liked it, others did not. But the truth found its way to some hearts and lodged there.

From here I made my way to West Poland, or Maguire Hill, driving directly to Bro. John Maguire's. Here I found a pilgrim's home, with warm Christian greeting. In this place I found a good number of disappointed, disconsolate, lonely ones, not meeting together. I stayed here some time, visiting, holding meetings, getting them from a "shut door" to an open one. I well remember my first meeting held there. It was at Bro. Jordan's. Here I found Elder Joseph Turner. He came to the meeting. I did my best to show them that we were not left in darkness; that the daylight had not gone, but the sun still shone upon us. Laboring with them faithfully, I had the joy of seeing them come out of that cast-down condition and take hold of the Lord God of Israel. A new state of things was seen, and cheerful countenances appeared among the believing ones, and blessed seasons followed. This was one of the strongholds of Adventism. I stayed with them until my attachments became so strong for them that I could hardly tear myself away. The Maguires, Jordans, Libbys and many others are still remembered with affectionate regard, though some of them sleep, waiting for the trumpet's voice, calling them to the great gathering of all the ransomed of the Lord.

Leaving West Poland very reluctantly, I made my way to Portland, where I had previously visited and made the acquaintance of the sainted Deacon Pearson and his family. They all had fully fallen in love with the heavenly tidings. Here I spent some days, preaching, visiting and praying with the people as the way opened. Many needed comforting here as everywhere else, for it was a time of severe trial. Here in this visit I found that good and eminent Methodist preacher L. C. Stockman, full of the faith for which he was excommunicated by the Maine Methodist Conference. But he "kept the faith," and finished his course, and died in the hope of life at the coming of his Lord, whose gospel and coming he so fearlessly preached. I visited him in his last sickness. "Ready to be offered," he waited the yielding up of his life to Christ. He sleeps until the morning, when them that sleep in Jesus will awake with him.

After finishing my labor in Portland, I made my way towards home. On coming into Portsmouth, N. H., just before night, I thought I would look up some of my Advent brethren. I had never been here, so I knew no one in the city. I rode along on the main street and made a number of inquiries for Adventists, but could get no knowledge of any, they not being known by those of whom I inquired. At length seeing a fine looking, portly man on the sidewalk, I drove up towards him and said, "Can you, sir, tell me where I can find an Adventist?" He hesitated as if my language was a foreign one. I then said, "They are sometimes called Millerites."

At this he seemed relieved, and quickly replied, "Oh, yes, there is Colonel Drown; he is the head Millerite here. I can tell you where he lives." By his direction I went directly to the Colonel's house. Ringing the bell, a nice-looking woman presented herself. I asked, "Is Colonel Drown, the head Millerite in?" I saw she did not relish the title, but at length said that he would be in at six o'clock; then I could see him. At the time she named I called again at the door. It was opened by an elderly man of a commanding look. I said, "Is this Col. Drown?" He said it was. I then told him who I was, and why I called upon him. He asked, "Are you the man that called here this afternoon and designated me as the head Millerite?" I said, "I am the man." He seemed disturbed; but when I told him how I ascertained his name, and described the sort of man who gave him the title of "head Millerite," he smiled, and said, "I know who he was; it was Judge Blank. That is just like him." That eased it off, and I had a welcome. After supper he went with me to the place fitted up just before for meetings; and also introduced me to that godly woman Sister Foster. Before I left the city I found a goodly number of Advent believers, but they were greatly discouraged, and waiting for further light. It was not long before they rallied, and with the blessing of the great God built them a nice chapel, and had it well filled.

After leaving there, I made my way through Exeter, Lawrence, Lowell, having good seasons with the believers in each place. Was welcomed home after an absence of three months.

CHAPTER XIII.

Changes, with a New Time

I**N** those few years after our great disappointment, by searching the Scriptures the faith of many respecting the final condition of the lost underwent a great change. We learned that instead of being alive eternally, and suffering in torment, the wicked would be destroyed, root and branch, and be as though they had not been. We came to see by the word of God that man was entirely mortal; that through Jesus Christ alone immortality was to be had; and believing on him was the only way of obtaining eternal life. This view, however, was not taken by all who had looked for the Lord, and so there was a division, the larger number of Adventists believing in the non-immortality of man. This division continues; but as a people, in looking for the Lord, we are united, having the same love for the coming of the King in his beauty to raise the dead and fit up the earth for the eternal abode of the immortalized saints.

Through these years I continued to travel in all directions in the several States, having all the calls I could attend to, and often more. I attended a score of Campmeetings in Mass., Maine, New Hampshire, Rhode Island and elsewhere, witnessing as before, the wonderful work of salvation by the preaching of this gospel of the kingdom, to be preached as a witness to all nations until the end. While there was a difference of opinion relative to the nature of man, and the very time of the Lord's coming, the gospel of Christ never was proclaimed with more clearness, and believed more firmly.

About 1850 a paper was started in Hartford, Conn., called *The Advent Watchman*. This advocated the unconsciousness of the dead, the destruction of the wicked and the soon coming of Christ. It was edited by David Crary, W. S. Campbell; Eld. Timothy Cole and others having a hand in it. It freely discussed the subject of life and death, and the return of Christ at hand. The "Six Sermons" of George Storrs, and his paper, the *Bible Examiner*, contained all the main arguments in favor of the unconsciousness of the dead, and the final destruction of the ungodly at the judgment. The doctrine of eternal life only through Christ had become prominent among us at this time and was being believed by many.

About this time there began to be a movement toward fixing upon another date for the Lord to come, and arguments from the Bible and chronology began to be rehearsed and printed. The year 1854 was the time indicated. Elder J. Couch and F. H. Berrick published a book, giving their reasons for expecting the advent in the above year; and this with other printed matter, preaching and special meetings produced great excitement in many quarters of the land.

Soon after this Elder Miles Grant began to be known among us. We then seemed to come to a new era. This time movement brought into existence the *World's Crisis*, which, while it advocated that time for the Lord to come, did not cease to promulgate the great truths of revelation when the time looked to had passed. The expectation of meeting the Lord in 1854, and the preaching it was attended with the blessing of God to many, who date their convictions and conversion at that time. Many also came into the faith in consequence of hearing the prophecies then preached. Like the going forth in 1844, it had its great results, which are best known by the heavenly ones above. There was the spirit, zeal, enthusiasm in the '54 movement that was witnessed in '44. They sang:

> "In eighteen hundred fifty-four,
> We will go home to die no more."

The last great meeting held was in Exeter, N. H. This was attended by all the leading brethren in the '54 time. There was great disappointment in the passing of this time, but it did not effect the body as that of 1844 did. The publication of the *Advent Watchman* ceased with 1854, and in its place was published the *Christian Reformer and Signs of the Times*. Joseph Turner was proprietor and editor. This was a free paper in which to discuss the doctrines of the Bible, especially the non-immortality of the soul. It was ably edited. This paper continued one year.

The *World's Crisis*, which had until then been published in Lowell, was removed to Boston, and became the leading paper of the larger Advent body, and is still its organ. Its first permanent editor was Jonas Merriam. Afterward Miles Grant, then John Couch, and now E. A. Stockman. While there had been some falling off of numbers in the body during these years, there were additions that more than made up for those who had gone aside, or left us. As a people our influence has been mightily felt, and the truth in relation to man and his final redemption has spread and prevailed greatly over the error of those days. The anti-Bible theology of the day is being shaken, and in many cases gives way to the teachings of the gospel. From this time, 1854-55, my labors were continuous.

I spent much of my time in this State (Mass.), meeting my appointments regularly as the Lord opened the way and helped me on. There was no lack of work for the years that followed. New Hampshire was a field in which I found much work, meeting often with good working brethren in the ministry in that State. Some of them, yea, many there, have left the walls of Zion, and lie in the valley. It was back there among the hills that the Lord poured out his Spirit upon both preacher and people marvelously.

I attended the first Campmeeting at Wilbraham. Met there the most of our pioneer and leading preachers. This meeting was a most remarkable one. The power of God was in the preaching and all that was said. The praying and singing, with the word dispensed, were mighty in the salvation of sinners and the comforting of saints. Long to be remembered was that meeting. A mighty impetus was given to the work of the Spirit at that great gathering. Converts to Christ and to the faith were made there by scores.

CHAPTER XIV.

Experience and Deep Affliction.

HERE have been some all through these years who have thought we would know the very time when the Lord would come. Some have fixed on one time and some on another, and these times have been freely discussed among us, as a people, in our papers, and publicly in our meetings. But the prophetic pen has not erred. That says, no one knoweth the time—the day or the hour—only "when he is near." This is enough to know—"even at the doors."

The winter of 1860-61 I spent in Biddeford, Me. This was the commencement of the Advent Church there. Brn. Libby and Hyde were the only believers there who could be depended upon at first. They made great sacrifices in sustaining a meeting; but the Lord had access to the hearts of some others, and our meetings increased in numbers and interest, while members were added to the church. A permanent meeting was established, which resulted in their building a chapel, with a prosperous church to worship therein.

We now come to the time of the war, on account of the Southern Rebellion. I had a son-in-law, Henry Moore, among the soldiers at the front. His wife, my daughter Adelaide, was left with me. While he was away she sickened, and on the 24th of May, 1863, fell asleep in Jesus. Her disease was bronchial consumption. She had a good hope, and gave good evidence that her life was hid with Christ in God, and that when Christ appears, she will appear in glory. So we did not mourn as those who have no hope. Our hope sustained us in this time of trial.

The elements of war are detrimental to the gospel of peace and good will to man. There was at this time a concentration of effort made to keep the keynote of Adventism heard, and the signs of the times seen by the people. We visited again our Eastern State, and did missionary work all the way up the Penobscot River, and had good success in sowing the good seed. Attended Campmeetings in the State, and itinerated with Brn. Brewer, Hemenway, Berrick and Ross. Those were days when prayer prevailed, and the truth took hold. Then self-denial was practiced, and a holy people was found who knew God.

I often visited Kennebunkport. Here was a strong company of believers, and they were not dwarfs in faith, but pronounced Adventists, full of the fire of the gospel of the kingdom. The light which they had in them shone out, and it was only to get them together, and there would be a flame with a heat that would anihilate all the chills one might have about him.

About this time (1862) there began to be a talk of establishing a permanent Campmeeting in Eastern Mass. Deciding upon the best place was to be done. The place finally fixed upon was Alton Bay, N. H., and in 1863 the first Campmeeting was held there. I was much interested in this movement; was present in the preparation of the ground, being one of the Campmeeting Committee. The Lord smiled upon the work from the first, even before the dedication of the grove. The first meeting brought fruit to his honor and glory. The establishment of this Campmeeting was a most successful means of spreading the light and truth as they shine forth in the word of God. From cloth tents the camp grew into cottages, but of the roughest kind, for those who built them did not expect to use them long. So the first built were in accordance with the faith of their builders; and some stand there at this day as a monument of the faith of that day.

About this time I was afflicted by the sickness of my wife. But she got able to attend the Campmeeting at Alton Bay in 1865. But little time passed after our return home, before Sarah, then my only daughter, and who was with us at the Campmeeting, was taken sick with typhoid fever, and died suddenly, leaving us alone. She was twenty years old. This was a sad bereavement. But the dear child fell asleep in Jesus, which gave us comfort in the midst of affliction deep. Soon after Sarah's death, my wife being lonely, I took her with me to Lynn, and she did not return to Groton. Presently we sought a home in Salem, and moved there. Sold our house in Groton, to live there no more. Soon after our removal to Salem, my wife grew more feeble and continued to fail until Jan. 1866, when she, too, fell asleep in Jesus, and was laid beside her children in Groton. The funeral service was attended by Elder Rufus Wendell. This left me in Salem, my son and his wife, living with me. I had a home, a pleasant home, but I was sad, bereft and lonely. But sustaining grace was given me in all my afflictions. I found a church of Adventists in Salem, with whom I worshipped when at home. Elder Rufus Wendell was the pastor.

CHAPTER XV.

Sick, and Miraculously Healed.

AFTER about two years of loneliness in traveling in the ministry among the hills and through the valleys of a number of States, I at length found a companion in the person of Sr. Caroline A. Ryder, of Chelsea, Mass., who after much solicitude and seeking for wisdom, which is profitable to direct, consented to unite her interests with mine, and care for me. So on Aug. 27, 1867, we were united in lawful marriage, I taking her to Salem with me. This was a happy union in the Lord, a union of two of like precious faith. Now again I had a helper and comforter in the gospel; a blessing in domestic life. This was a new epoch in my history, and I fully believe it was in the ordering of God. We soon came to Chelsea, where she had resided with her first husband; and this has been our permanent home for more than twenty years of love, happiness and peace. In these years, as a helper to me, she has been second to my Lord.

On Sept. 28th, 1871, the new chapel built in Chelsea was dedicated. Elder John Couch preached the dedication sermon. The church here did most nobly in this work; and this building, erected at a sacrifice, has been one of the most useful chapels anywhere; not only for the use of the church, but for Conferences, meetings of the business associations of the body ever since its erection.

In July 1870, I attended an important tent meeting held in Providence, R. I. It was in the Mass. mission tent, under the charge of Enoch Morrill. The tent was located on a hill in the southern part of the city. This meeting was a most prosperous and blessed one. It created a great stir in the city, which told to the advantage of the truth. There was considerable opposition to the Bible doctrine of immortality only through Christ, but the result was, that by the five weeks' meeting there, a church was afterwards formed, and a chapel built, now called the Hammond St. Advent Church and Chapel.

In 1873, I went again to Rutland, Vt., and spent some time with the church there. I made my home with Bro. Nahum Green and family. He was formerly a deputy sheriff; had been converted under the preaching of Elder M. Grant. The family had been brought to Christ and into the faith of his soon coming. It was blessed to find such a home. I was here two months or more, and by visiting and preaching a good work was done in the church; full meetings with increasing interest when I left. Praise the Lord.

From here I went to Castleton Vt. and had the pleasure of meeting there Bro. and Sr. Mathewson, and speaking to the people there. Before this a sister in Middleton had written me three times to come there and give the alarm. This was fifteen miles from Rutland. So after I returned to Rutland, I took Bro. Green's team and rode out to the place where the sister who had written to me lived. I found that she was the only person there who fully believed "our report." She found me a place to stay, and got the Methodist house for two or three lectures. The people came out well to hear. I gave them the coming of the Lord, and what he was coming for, which made quite a talk throughout the village. I left them discussing the subject with their minister and among themselves. How many converts I made, I know not. They gave me where I put up a good-sized cake of maple sugar, which I on my return gave to Bro. Green for the use of his team, while I kept the blessing of God which I got by going. I could but praise the Lord for his wonderful goodness in giving me health to be in the field and able to use the sword of the Spirit, which is the word of God.

Between 1873-75 I visited and preached in four or five different states, attending campmeetings, conferences and tentmeetings, and witnessed the power of God in bringing men to see the need of salvation by the Holy Spirit, and to accept of the terms thereof, and be made new. This paid for solicitude, self-denial and labor. The coming in of 1875 found me in a debilitated condition physically, from overwork.

In February I visited New Bedford, spending two Sundays, filling the desk and doing some visiting of the sick, who were very low—Bro. Lawrence and some others. On the second Sunday evening, after the meeting, I was partially paralyzed, but did not then know what the matter was with me. I kept up as best I could, and the next day Bro. Irish came home to Chelsea with me, where I arrived in a sad condition. All was immediately done for me that could be. What made my sickness more afflictive was, Lizzie Ryder, our only daughter, was sick with consumption, and nigh unto death. I did my best to keep up and help my wife to bear her burden. But I was nearly helpless. April 9th Lizzie died, falling asleep in Jesus, leaving us in a sad condition: wife mourning for her only child, and I so palsied as not to know hardly anything. I was put in bed, and was then without feeling, and unconscious most of the time, not knowing my nearest friends around me. The brethren came in to cheer us and pray for me, but I knew them not only at times. The doctors came in and consulted. They gave no hope of life, and said nothing could be done. A solemn time; the only hope there was, was in him "who healeth all our diseases." Prayers now went up in earnest for my recovery. *My wife in this extremity obtained the assurance that I would live, and like Hezekiah of old have fifteen years added to my life!* This gave others hope. After she obtained the evidence from the Lord that I would live, I immediately began to come out of the condition in which I had been nearly three months, in an almost paralyzed state, with but little consciousness at any time. When I began to come to myself everything looked strange and as if I had never before seen them. The most of my friends had given me up, but the Lord heard prayer, and I was made to live. Here was surely the manifestation of his power to heal when all human help failed.

The following is taken from the *World's Crisis*, written by the Editor during my sickness :

"Bro. L. Boutelle is very sick, doubtless unto

death. He has had one or two shocks of paralysis, which have completely broken his nervous system, and every organ of the body seems to have lost its vitality. He is mentally and physically sinking into death. He is very rapidly failing, and if the Lord does not interpose his power to stay the disease, he must very soon sleep the dreamless sleep.

"When he is conscious he is very happy, and praises God heartily and constantly. There seems to be a hallowed, sacred influence in his presence. It is sad to see one of our most faithful and beloved brethren in the ministry, who has so nobly and successfully defended the great and important truths of the gospel, sinking down at his post; but his armor is all on, and the last glances of his eye watching the strategetical movements of the enemies of Christ.

"But there is a silver lining to this dark cloud; for he exhibits the heavenly characteristics of sanctified, Christianized humanity. He manifests no interest in conversing upon common subjects; but when the coming of Christ, the resurrection of the dead, the signs of the times, and the blessedness of the coming kingdom are referred to, he invariably arouses, like an old soldier at the sound of martial music, and calls into action all the sinking, vital forces, in expressions of joyful praise and triumphant expectation.

"We said to him, 'The trees are putting forth. We know that summer is nigh.' His eye brightened, and with emphatic and measured sentences he said, 'Yes; that is so. "So likewise ye,—when ye shall see—all these things,—know that *it* is near,—even at the doors."' He then, with a very broken voice, rapturously sung—

> 'Roll swifter round, ye wheels of time,
> And bring the welcome day.'

Again he broke out, with an energy which was beyond his own, and sung—

> 'In that bright world no tears will flow;
> Death—'

and stopped, as if he had come to a gulf which had not been passed, and then with a falling cadence said, very impressively, 'Blessed — rest, — thrice blessed rest.' So sink good men down into death's undisturbed *rest*. J. C."

My health was most miraculously restored, so that by the July following I was working as usual in the vineyard of the Lord. And to the praise and glory of his name I write this. The fifteen years have been added, and more; and I have occupied those years in the service of my Master, and still am ready to do all that he demands of me.

> Still in the vineyard, let me faithful be,
> Living and laboring ever, Lord, for Thee.
> Not till Thou comest let my work be done;
> Then I would see Thee and possess the crown.

CHAPTER XVI.

Health Restored.　A Neighbor Quieted.

AFTER this new lease of life by divine healing, I had a new inspiration; and I felt a greater responsibility as my strength and vitality increased. Now I was able to labor as extensively as ever, and fill my place in evangelical work, not missing one of my appointments on Sundays, or meetings at other times during the following year.

On my next birthday, my twin brother, with his family visited me, with other relatives. This was the 4th of May, 1876. More than a score of friends came and dined with us, and it was a most pleasant and profitable time. I was still able to fill my appointments about home, and itinerated in different States, and the Lord smiled upon me in my effort to spread the light and truth.

I visited again New Hampshire, Maine, Connecticut, and also Pennsylvania. I was much encouraged and blessed in seeing the work of God prosper where I went. I saw an increase of faith in many places relative to the soon coming of the Lord; and many becoming convinced that life and immortality can only be obtained through Christ; that destruction awaits the wicked, and not eternal conscious being in torment. Still preaching and visiting the sick and poor is my mission, and this I have accomplished as I have had strength and ability.

I have attended many funerals, and comforted those who have mourned. Have married my share of those who have entered domestic life. And now in this added period of my life, I am more and more desirous of fulfilling my part of the prophetic work. Blessings are crowding themselves upon me and mine. We drink alike at the same unfailing fountain; and home is the oasis in this world's desert, when home is what it should be. It is made no less sweet by bidding those of like precious faith and hope to enter our circle and feel welcome. We have learned that true Christianity is to live for others' good; that the poor and destitute, even if they are our enemies, should find in our hearts and houses a place and sympathy. No one should be turned away who comes to us for help. We should remember the words of inspiration: "For none of us liveth to himself." A Christian home is the sweetest place on the earth. The parental home should be the most delightful spot that children could find. The sweetening of divine grace should be had in every domestic circle. This makes a happy family and a cheerful home. A father of a family should have the gospel religion, and by prayer, good words and works secure the blessing of the heavenly Father upon his household. God is love, and his government is administered in love; and the government of every family should be in love. The law of God is comprehended in this: "Love thy neighbor as thyself." This principle lived out, and there would be a check to the voice of slander; all difficulties would be healed between men, and many evils remedied. This gospel of good will was heralded by the heavenly host, as they shouted, "Glory to God in the highest, and on earth peace and good will toward men." It is this good will toward men that often makes friends of enemies. To illustrate this divine principle I will here relate some of my experience.

I once had a neighbor, who when he became my neighbor, people said we should always be in a quarrel, he was so exacting and unscrupulous. We drew water from the same well, it being on the line between us. I had no fear of any difficulty with my neighbors, for I had learned that love begets love, and that some people always had good neighbors, while others did not. Whenever the bucket or rope got out of order I would see it righted, and all went well, for he would inquire the cost, and say he would fix it the next time; so I saw it was working well. At length, one day, my boy told me that my near neighbor claimed that I had some of his land, as by a bound-mark between us. I thought nothing of it until one day, after getting home from a preaching tour, I took my hoe and went into my garden to hoe my potatoes. I saw that my neighbor was in his garden doing the same thing. Presently he came over into my garden, and going to the further side began to dig. After a short time he called me and said, "I have found the bound-mark between us;" pointing to a small stone about three feet in upon my land, "I think that's it," said he. I then said, "I think the fence is on the line, but if you think this is the true bound, put down your mark, and you may move the fence to it." He took his hoe and went back into his garden. I heard no more about the "bound-mark," living by him ten years after this. The gospel rule is the great remedy for overcoming evil.

My health continued, so that I began the new year with good courage and a fresh supply of added strength. Besides having work near home, I was called often away. I visited once more Rutland, Addison, and Bristol, Vt. Preached the gospel of the coming kingdom in these places, comforting the believers, and entreating others to hasten to the fountain, and drink of the living water and live. And still onward I pressed, as the years came and went. I was still running my rounds to feed the flock of God, of which the Holy Ghost has made me overseer, deriving comfort and courage by the blessings conferred upon me in my efforts put forth in weakness, but in faith and with a consolation and good hope.

An event of deep interest to me occurred this year which I cannot well omit mentioning. My twin brother Calvin and his wife had enjoyed wedded life a half century; and by the desire of their children, relatives and friends they were to celebrate the anniversary of fifty years of married life, by a gathering at their house in Townsend, Mass. On that day a tent was spread, near their home, in which a dinner was laid for the company. I had been selected to preside and make an address. As this was the wish of all, I consented to sit at the head of the table, and after the repast speak to the company as the occasion demanded. The following is the address:

"My Dearly Beloved Brother, Sister, Relatives and Friends,—By the mercies of God we are called together here to-day, to bring to mind the former days, as well as to celebrate with you the fiftieth year of your married life, or Golden Wedding. But few in wedded life are permitted to dwell thus long together; and it is by the goodness of God that you have outlived the generation of your childhood, and have the pleasure of being surrounded by your children, grandchildren, relatives and friends. And even to-day there would be but little to cheer and encourage, were it not for the memory of the past and the prospect of the future. We get comparatively little as we are crowded rapidly on with life's changes, only as memory lingers delightfully or sorrowfully upon the past, and we anticipate the future by hopeful promise. This makes up the most of human life. If our effort or desire fails we faint not, but catch the next chance with determined vigor, remembering, 'Where there's a will, there's a way.' Thus, by the inspiration of hope, we meet all the storms of life, and struggle with a grasp that will overcome almost every obstacle we find in our way.

Things have greatly changed since we were boys. Then we all went to one meeting. The old Puritan religion answered for all the honest-hearted. The one minister preached on the hill, and his dog, on the pulpit stairs, kept away all intruders! The gospel heat—with a few foot stoves for aged sisters—was supposed to be all that was neccessary for physical health or spiritual fervor. All went to meeting then. Large families could be seen in the sanctuary, rain or shine, cold or hot. Galleries crowded! All reverently worshiping one God! And the seats of the pews so arranged on hinges that when the minister said 'Amen,' they would all respond with an unmistakable relish. Bonnets, hats, and clothing seemed to be waterproof then. The preparatory lecture was not forsaken. This was fifty years ago!

Then we were not obliged to bolt the doors to keep out tramps, thieves, seducers, or murderers. If one was out with large sums of money on his person, by day or by night, no suspicion of foul play. Defalcations, forgery, or clandestinely taking monies entrusted to one's care, was not expected in the church or ministry fifty years ago. *This*, after all that can be said, seems like the golden age.

Look back to our peers—the Adames, the Spauldings, the Gileses, Wires, Blogetts, Wilders, Walkers, Balls, Boutelles, and a host of the Puritan stamp, firm in the faith, all moving on harmoniously, with the Rev. David Palmer giving them the divinely inspired word of God, unadulterated by human wisdom! This was fifty years ago! I freely admit a progression both literary and scientific; but how is it with the Christian moral standard? But I forbear.

Fifty years ago, you took your Thirza to this sacred spot, the old homestead of Deacon Giles—not Deacon Giles of the distillery reputation, but the good old Puritan deacon—and this very soil has been consecrated by prayer and fasting! Honest dealing had been inaugurated here before you stepped upon the soil. The golden rule was the deacon's rule. It was not, 'Get what you can, and keep what you get.' I well remember that my father made his family shoes with the understanding that a bushel of corn or rye paid for a pair of shoes; and when corn brought $2.50 instead of $1.00, it only paid for a pair of shoes with Deacon Giles; and when it brought only 75 cts. per bushel, it paid for a pair of shoes with Deacon Boutelle. And thus should the moral honesty of the old farm be kept up, till the mighty hand of our God shall bring it back to its primitive purity by a restitution.

The celebration of this important event, seems to concentrate the struggles and pleasures of more than half a century of domestic life. It is not of common occurrence. You, my dear brother and sister, are an exception to the rule.

You are a favored couple. And the goodness of

God calls upon you for gratitude and thanksgiving for the blessings of a long, happy, wedded life, to a good old age! Living by permission, on borrowed time! Let the closing up scenes of life's drama be spent in the service of our Christ, who is soon to appear; that you may be able to say with the apostle, 'Whether we live, we live unto the Lord; whether we die, we die unto the Lord: whether we live or die, therefore, we are the Lord's.'"

After the address I read the following poem, which I had written for the occasion. Subsequently, at the request and expense of the friends, both were printed and circulated among those interested in the golden wedding of my brother and wife. That was on May 13th, 1880. My brother and I had just passed our 74th birthday, that being the 4th of May, nine days previous.

THE POEM.

"We now will look at scenes left far behind,
 Bringing the family record fresh to mind.
 No farther in the past, to-day you'll hear,
 Then eighteen hundred six—eventful year.
 That was the time, the people say,
 A strange surprise, the fourth of May.
 A good old deacon lived in town,
 And to his stock two boys were born.
 Luther and Calvin they were named,
 If not in grace, none could be blamed.
 Parents and neighbors did rejoice.
 Among them all it was their choice.

The history, thus far, is not mine;
For I remember not the time.
It must have been long time ago,
Or the surprise I'd surely know.
I remember well, in after days,
I met the boys, in school and plays.
These boys grew up, perhaps not smart;
In mischief they could act their part.
Their childhood days soon took their flight—
Their parents taught them what was right.
The deacon would have them in a row;
For Sundays they must to meeting go.
Their way was through the chestnut field—
To this temptation they would yield:
Sometimes they'd stop and pick them up,
Then they'd to drink the bitter cup.
The deacon was the tithing man:
For Sabbath-breaking to him they ran.
'Mischievous boys!' all join and say,
'The deacon should not let them stray.'
But the deacon did the best he could:
He prayed, and taught them to be good.
Into the church they must be brought,
And theologically taught.
Thus, with best wishes of parent's heart,
On life's rough journey they must start.
Childhood and youth are left behind,
And manhood's prospects fill the mind.
Our father's house and parents' care
Must now be left—life's toils to bear;
Do for one's self the best you can
To gain a living, and be a man.

For domestic life, desire grows strong:
To have a wife could not be wrong.
God had taught us, it was not good
To toil alone for daily food.

So now inclined to look around,
To see if the prize could not be found;
Now comes the time of hope and fear,
And stern research from year to year.
At length the long sought comes in sight:
Both fall in love—and all works right.
Consent of parents is freely had,
And all hearts are at once made glad.
The day is set, the friends must come
To see the twain by law made one.
The parson now is called, to say,
'Husband and wife are you, this day:
What God hath joined, so let it be;
Let no man put asunder thee.'
We now come to your wedding day,
The thirteenth of the smiling May:
That blissful bridal day, you know,
To-day, was fifty years ago.
The voyage of life was then begun,
Your hopes and interests were one.
New scenes of pleasure and of bliss,
Such as united hearts could wish.
Your prospect bright—new friends you greet,.
And married life to you is sweet.
At length, to make all hearts rejoice,
The cheering sound—an infant's voice!
No regret with parents to hear the cry—
The stern command was 'multiply.'
So this is in prophetic line;
Not to obey would be a crime.
The cradle now begins to rock
The firstling of a little flock.
Another! and another, still!
The cradle has its constant fill.
Battle commenced, it must be fought,
If other plans are brought to nought.
The prattlings, all, dear souls! they share

A loving mother's tender care.
They fret and scold, they laugh and cry,
And, for your life, you can't tell why.
But then you take it with good will,
For you can't keep the darlings still.
Sometimes your patience has to yield;
But soon sound reason takes the field.
Thus married life has quickly run—
Sorrows and pleasures in all that's done.
Correction, discipline, on they go
To manhood: thus the children grow.
But still their parents' cares and fears
Follow them on, to riper years.
If they prove faithful, good, and true,
Nothing more pleasing they could do.

By God's great goodness, grace divine,
You've lived together so long a time.
Such blessing is granted but to few,
And thankful hearts to Him are due.
Your children and friends—so very dear,—
To-day have come, to greet you here.
Your children are your chief delight;
They'll seek to make your burdens light.
Life's remnant will be quickly run,
While you will pray, 'Thy kingdom come'!
While warring through this mortal race,
You'll need the power of saving grace.
Humiliating, to know we must,
In a few days, be turned to dust!
'The living know that they must die,'
And, doomed to *hades*, there must lie.
But then, the hope the Gospel gives
Brings from the grave, and makes men live!
Christ tasted death—rose the third day:
So, in the grave men cannot stay.
The words of Christ are not in vain;

'If a man dies, he'll live again.'
Christ Jesus died—He's now alive;
So all Christ's sleepers will revive.
Then in His likeness they will be,
All clothed with immortality.
This 'blessed hope,' while on the way,
Should cheer your hearts, from day to day.
And when our blessed Lord shall come,
He'll bid you to a welcome home:
Sweet home! beyond the reach of strife;
The new-earth home—with endless life.

The children here—both one and all—
I hope will hear the gracious call;
That they may not be turned away
From life, in the great coming day.
Grandchildren, friends, to us so dear,
I hope to Christ they will give ear;
The pleasant path of wisdom take,
And with the good their journey make.

This is a day of mirth and cheer
With loving friends around you here.
But soon alas! again we part,
And separate with saddened heart:
The good, at last, with Christ shall meet,
Salvation's story to repeat;
While endless ages roll along
Redemption's story shall be our song."

CHAPTER XVII.

Healing in Answer to Prayer.

THE following year, 1881, was a very successful year of labor in the Lord's vineyard, for my strength was according to the demands for work. I had all that I could do. My mission work accumulated on my hands, and consequently my time was all taken up in my specific work; so when the yearly bound was reached, it seemed but a day; for the more one is engaged in the work of saving men, and the older he grows, the faster time seems to run.

Thus 1881 and 1882 passed, bringing me and all nearer the judgment. The seasons of blessing, of happiness and sorrow on life's journey, once passed through, are forever in the past. In my labors, public and private, at home and abroad, I have had the favor of God and my brethren. They have been lovingly kind to me in all my infirmities and weaknesses. Much of my life has been spent in excitement, with an interest, sometimes intense in that which seemed to me to be for the glory of God and the best good of all. I have kept a horse which has enabled me to do more visiting than I otherwise could have done. In these calls of mercy upon the poor and sick, the isolated saints, there are sweet remembrances of special blessings bestowed upon them. They linger in the memory, and increase gratitude to God. I could chronicle many like the following:

I was in Lynn one time and felt a drawing to visit Bro. Sederquist. Found him sick, and with a terrible cough and difficult breathing. Our visit was short, but a blessed one. I cheered him as much as I could with the "blessed hope," had a free season in prayer, calling upon God in his behalf, asking that he might have immediate relief. I came away, feeling well. The next time I saw Bro. S. he told me that the difficulty left him immediately after I left him, and he was able to attend to his duties, and on Sunday to preach as usual. To God, the Healer, we gave all the glory. These special seasons of relief and healing have not been uncommon. I have witnessed them all the way in my preaching experience. Nothing makes one feel so small, weak and dependent as to have God work his wonders through our agency.

I at one time preached in Portsmouth, N. H. I put up with that sainted couple, Bro. and Sister Chase. Bro. C. came home Saturday evening very fatigued and feeling ill. Sunday morning, however, he went to the meeting, but had trouble in returning on account of an attack of rheumatism. This kept him at home the rest of the day. On my return from the evening meeting I found him in a state of great anxiety, fearing he would not be able to go to his work the next day, as he had work that was promised, and which was necessary to be done at once. I comforted him what I could, and got down and asked my heavenly Father in the name of his Son to remember and heal this godly man; to ease his pain, make him limber, so that he could fulfill his promise by being at his work. I retired for rest. I arose in the morning before seven o'clock, but Bro. Chase was not to be seen; he had gone to his work all right. He afterwards assured me and his brethren that his going to his work the next day was in answer to prayer. This is proof that God is the same that the Bible represents him to be, a prayer-hearing God.

I was once called to the bedside of a sick lady, a member of the Congregational Church. Her disease was consumption. In conversation with her, I found her in a state of reconciliation to her Saviour. But one thing troubled her. She had a lingering desire for life. She wanted to live that she might do more good. She was anxious to know if that desire was wrong. I comforted her by giving her examples from the Bible, where good men wanted to live longer, assuring her that after fourscore years in life, with faith in Christ, I wanted to live longer. This greatly comforted the dying one, and lighted up her last hours; and in hope she fell asleep in Jesus.

These examples of God's goodness to his people, comforting and healing the wounded spirit, are manifest in every age. Let us recognize him in these things, and give him the glory. I see as I advance in life the same good hand guiding me along the way, and through the last-day perils, both at home and abroad; I lacking no good thing. I am satisfied with my salary, "What is right, I will give you." My bread and water are made sure. Thus faring as the Lord directs, I still look for the "blessed hope," and do all I can to have others look for the same.

I see by my jottings, that 1883 passed as the previous year did, I going here and there in the gospel field, telling the story of salvation, and calling upon all to come to the great Physician and be cured of the disease of sin, and live forever.

I visited again Addison and Bristol, Vt., laboring

five weeks with the faithful friends of Jesus there, and finding my labor not in vain in the Lord. So there, as well as in all other places, I could rejoice with those who rejoiced, and weep with those wept. In Christ Jesus I can do all things, suffer all things and be content. But it is all of grace.

Through the following winter I was kept in the field, able to preach every Sunday, beside working in protracted meetings, officiating at funerals, visiting the sick and dying. Thus in good health under my lengthened lease of life, keeping myself in the faith, and being kept alive by the power of God, salvation seemed the great thing to be thought of, and proclaimed; the only thing worth seeking, the only thing that should be preached.

The years 1884 to 1887 passed with but little change in the manner of my life. The work was the same in the vineyard of the Lord. I did not tire in it. It was all for Christ, and he being with me helped me in every hard task. There was self-denial in leaving home and many comforts I could not get elsewhere, however kind my brethren and sisters all were. "There is no place like home"; but this must be left behind to preach the gospel of Christ to the world. During these years I revisited many places in the different States. In Maine I visited Bangor, Levant, and other places. In Vermont,

Rutland, Middleton, Addison, Bristol, with other towns. In Rhode Island, Bristol, Woonsocket and other places. In all my goings I was wonderfully preserved in health and from accidents, and considering my advanced age thus exposed, I am a wonder to myself.

CHAPTER XVIII.

Afflicted with Loss of Hearing.

WHEN I entered the year 1888, it was with the same expectation of being still useful in my calling, socially and in a public manner. The first Sunday in this year I preached in Farmington, N. H. The week following I attended a Conference in Boston, of the early believers of this faith. This was a blessed greeting of the old hands as well as of the new ones, who were all waiting for the coming Lord. Time moved on until Feb. 12, with an appointment for Sunday on my hands, and expecting to fulfill it. But alas! as I awoke in the morning, my wife spoke to me, but got no answer! Then again with the same result! Then I learned that while I slept I had lost my hearing. That was a sad morning for both myself and wife. I could see her lips move, but could hear no sound. This was almost too great a loss to be reconciled to. To be laid aside, and be of no use, socially or in any other way, was terrible to think of. I, who had for years been active in the work of proclaiming the gospel, now, when I wanted to preach it more than ever, and thus end my life—thus to be laid by and of no use, was truly afflictive. But reflecting upon the mercies of the past, I became more reconciled to my condition. But it stopped my labors for the time being, and as I thought of this, it was humiliating in the extreme. My social enjoyment at home and abroad was almost lost, and my work about ended, and I was left a kind of blank in the world. Saddening indeed was the thought. My condition caused me much meditation and prayer. To say "Thy will be done" caused me a great struggle; but I did say it. This was a relief. With others I prayed for healing, and felt an assurance that I should be relieved, and after a time I began to hear better, and for this I praised the Lord. In getting used to my condition, I became more reconciled to my lot. But not until May 4, 1889 did I venture to speak again publicly; then only to attend funerals and preach a little.

This commenced another epoch in my history. I was sorely afflicted, but I could find no fault with my Lord and Master. He had been so good to me in the past, that ears to hear or not, I would serve him the best I could and trust him the remnant of my life. With this resolution formed by the aid of the Spirit, I was made comfortably passive, and got along better than I thought I could. My infirmity seemed to lessen, so that during the latter part of the year, I could preach some, attend my favorite Campmeeting, and with my wife visit again my Vermont friends in a tarry of four weeks, and preach some to them. This with Sunday work in Everett, Mass. finished up the year. So being able to preach some, attend to my household affairs, I entered upon another year.

The new year comes in upon us almost imperceptibly. The past with its events are forever gone. The present finds me in good courage, and with comfortable health; determined by grace given me to persevere under the good care of my heavenly Father, who has been my support from the beginning of my service for him, so that I have lacked for nothing that was needed. And now with all my disabilities, I step along trusting in the one who never forsakes those who serve him, and depend upon him. While my public ministry has been much hindered by my infirmities, I have had something to do in ministerial labor. I have preached often this year. I have attended nine funerals, besides making many visits where the Lord seemed to lead me. Have written many letters to comfort the isolated ones, and the flock in general. My 83d birthday found me in quite good health.

I will here speak of an event which to me was an important one. It was the death of my twin brother, whom I have mentioned so many times in these sketches. He and myself were the last of Deacon John and Abagail Boutelle's nine children. In life, my brother and I had come along together, trained, when young, in the old theological school. While I afterwards left behind my early religious teachings, he held fast to his. But this did not hinder us from being twin brothers still. I did my best to have the one faith and hope in our twinship; but in this I failed, he clinging to his Puritan theology. In my last visit to his home, he told me that I had got his children into my faith, and he could not say it was not the true one. He always received me cordially, expressing a desire for my prayers when I left him. The first day of July, 1888, he fell asleep in Jesus, to wait the trumpet's call to judgment; when we all shall appear before the judgment-seat of Christ. July 3d, we attended his funeral. We then, with his family, after solemn services, committed him to the dust. "Dust thou art, and unto dust thou shalt return." The resurrection will find him where they laid him. Jesus said that all who are in their graves shall come forth. We left the home where he spent his days, and with sadness of heart, thought how all but myself of my father's family had gone down by death's cruel hand—I alone being left.

CHAPTER XIX.

Death in Family.   Visit to Vernon, Vt.

I NOW come to this year, 1890.   I am older, but with no less physical ability than one year ago.   Strange is the problem of life.   We grow older without giving it much thought; and if it were not that we counted the yearly bound-mark, we would not know how old we were.   The daily mercies and blessings which we could not live without, are often forgotten.   But the Lord don't forget us, though we may forget him.

We have had in our family until of late a very excellent woman, as a boarder. But she is no more with us, for she suddenly sickened and died. On the night of March 13, she called to my wife, who found her in great distress. I went for the doctor. He found her in a critical condition, with heart trouble. She was relieved, and seemed much better. Sunday, the 16th, she passed a comfortable day, but at 7 P. M. we were called to her bedside to hear her say a few words, and see her breathe her last, and fall asleep in Jesus. On the 20th the funeral services were held at my house, where the relatives and friends had gathered. By request I attempted to comfort them with the hope of a better life, by a resurrection from the dead. Her death in our house was a shock to us. She was a good woman, genial and kind; and although she did not see altogether as we did, her love for Christ made sweet our conversation and worship in the family.

On the 4th of May, 1890, I reached my eighty-fourth birthday in quite good health. It was Sunday, and there was to be a baptism of six converts to the faith. Our Pastor, Eld. N. P. Cook, with myself and a good number of our Chelsea Advent Church, went over to East Boston to baptismal waters, where a heavenly scene was witnessed. It was in the same manner that Jesus was baptized, and also the eunuch. There was a crowd of witnesses who came to behold the divine ordinance administered. The candidates came up out of water rejoicing in hope of a resurrection, foreshadowed by their baptism. In the afternoon I went to Everett and preached to the Advent Mission Church. It was a delightful birthday.

The last week in June, myself and wife visited

our relatives in Kennebunkport, Maine. From there we went to the Advent Campmeeting at Old Orchard, meeting there a goodly number of faithful ones looking for the Lord, longing for his coming. Returning home, both myself and wife found that the trip taken had done us good, both physically and spiritually. So we concluded to continue our journeyings. Accordingly in July we went to Worcester. There we visited Bro. and Sr. Couch and others taking and giving counsel in a gospel way, and comforting one another in the faith. On our way home we called upon our sainted Sr. Boody, who now lives in Cochituate with her son. On leaving, she invited us to accompany her to Alton Bay and accept a home with her in her cottage. This we talked over, and on reaching home wrote her that we would accept her kind offer and meet her in Boston. Starting July 25, we stopped at Farmington, N. H., over Sunday with Bro. Drew and family. Monday forenoon we reached the Bay, opened the cottage and soon made it home-like. This was my 27th annual visit to this consecrated and sacred spot. The 11th of Aug. we were obliged to return home. Our stay was delightful. I had health to preach three times, and came home refreshed.

We remained at home until the 28th of Aug., when we took the cars for Vermont. At 2 P. M. arrived at Rutland. After waiting two hours, we took a train for Castleton, where our friend Silas Giddings resides. He met us at the depot, and took us with his span to his country farm-house, where we were welcomed by the family. Here we tarried certain days. While here he took with his span of lively steeds, his family, my wife and myself to the Advent Campmeeting at Fairhaven. Here we spent two days, uniting most heartily with the lovers of Jesus and his coming in divine worship. We were now near the earthly home of Bro. William Miller, the first proclaimer of the near coming of Jesus our Lord. Here we met some of the old pioneers of this last gospel of the kingdom, and a number of the new advocates of the same hope. I had the pleasure of shaking hands with two of Bro. Miller's children, a son and a daughter, and really it seemed like what they used to call a Millerite meeting. Returning from the Fairhaven Campmeeting to Castleton, bidding Bro. Giddings and family good bye in the Lord, we went to Addison. Here we found a welcome in the mansion of Sr. Huldah N. Brevoort. Here we remained during our stay in A, with the exception that we visited Bro. Wm. S. Howden, in Bristol, during the time mentioned. We preached in Addison each Sunday during our stay there, in their consecrated chapel. We shall not forget the Advent band in Addison. Their history and names are written in the book of remembrance. They are a tried people, as all God's people are. But they hold fast, and none will take their crowns. Some of the old veterans still live; but if their Lord does not come soon, they will be among the sleepers.

Oct. 2, we left the little church in A. with strong prayers and tears, and took our last look of those mountain peaks, bidding all farewell for the present, and stepped on board the train for Boston. We came on with pleasant recollections, and at 6 P. M. reached the "Hub," and at our home in Chelsea in safety, and thankful to the God of all goodness, for his wonderful love and protection of us in our old age. This imperfect sketch is finished.

> This glimpse of my life, with its hopes and its fears,
> I've written from memory, at eighty-four years:
> It's experimental and doctrinal too;
> Though simple the narrative, yet it is true.
>
> L. B.

MISCELLANEOUS.

Divine Healing.

DIVINE healing is a Bible theme, and is found in both the Old and New Testament. God healed diseases in the old dispensation.

When Jesus was here he healed many of whatever disease they had. While he was with his disciples he gave them power over unclean spirits, and also power to heal the sick, and this power they had after he went away. The apostles demonstrated their faith in the promise of Christ, by laying their hands on the sick and seeing them healed. The promise connected with the commission found in Mark 16: 15, that "they should lay hands on the sick, and they should recover," has never been taken back by the Saviour. This is proved by the same having been done through all the gospel dispensation when the church has been spiritual and under the control of Christ. Now I understand that this promise holds good as long as the commission is given to those who are sent out to carry the gospel into all the world. Jesus says, "Lo, I am with you alway, *even unto the end of the world.*" This gives us the divine healing, as we find it mentioned in James, until Jesus comes.

And this has been no very infrequent thing among us, as a people; for at the beginning of the proclamation of this message of our Lord's soon coming, there was displayed the power of God in the miraculous healing of the sick. An account of the many cases of recovery from sickness by the prayer of faith among us, then and since if published would doubtless make a larger volume than this. Whenever the directions, given by James, are strictly followed, and healing faith possessed, there will be the healing power manifested. I witnessed many such cases in my early Advent experience; two of which I will relate.

In 1845 or ,46 I attended a Conference in the town of Brimfield, Mass. It was an out-door meeting, of great interest and power. At this meeting there was a good sister who had a bronchial trouble, and had lost her voice. I was well acquainted with her. It was with much difficulty that she could make any one understand her. She had an intense desire for the restoration of her voice, so that she might sing, pray and enjoy the meeting.

Believing in healing by prayer, she called upon the believing ones to pray for her that she might be healed. So we gathered for that purpose and called on the Lord according to his word. The power of the living God was there indeed. While we were praying, she began to shout and praise the Lord with her natural voice, and subsequently sang as in former times. During the meeting she did this, and returned home with the joy of one whom the Lord had graciously dealt with.

But there is a sequel to this. After her return home, her physician, hearing in regard to the restoration of her voice at the meeting, called on her. She related how her voice was restored, and gave God the glory. He at once began caviling, saying that the case was a very clear one on natural principles; that there was nothing miraculous about it. Talking in this manner for a time, the woman became bewildered, and her faith faltered. The result was that that very day she again became speechless. The doctor's dose of infidelity took effect; she pondering over the subject until her faith was destroyed, and she became sad and miserable.

At the meeting above-mentioned another was appointed to be held a few weeks in the future, but in another place. To this meeting she came, but with a downcast look. On meeting her, she clasped my hand with tears in her eyes, but no audible word could be heard. I said, "You have been unbelieving, and so have lost your voice again." She assented. After a day at this meeting, with weeping she made a request that they pray for her again. This was acceded to, and together we bowed before the Lord and prayed in her behalf. With deep repentance she whispered a promise that she would not disbelieve the Lord again if he would once more restore her voice. The prayer of faith was heard in heaven, and healing power came in answer. The afflicted one was able to praise the Lord aloud for his pardoning love and grace. This created a new interest in the meeting, and the Spirit of God ruled with great power in all hearts.

It may be asked by those who read this, if this sister kept her voice after this second restoration through prayer and faith. I can say, I saw her eight or ten years after this, and her voice was as natural and strong as before she lost it, and she was still using it for the glory of God. "The prayer of faith shall save the sick, and the Lord shall raise him up."

ANOTHER CASE OF HEALING

I will give one more case of the wonderful healing power of God which it was my lot to witness and be used by the Great Physician.

It was in a family I had often visited, living in the town of Brimfield, Mass. The name of the family was Hitchcock. A daughter by the name of Ann had for some time been sick, and all that could be done for her recovery had been done. Physicians had attended her, but she grew worse until all hope of her recovery was lost. She was a devoted follower of Jesus, and ready to live for him or fall asleep in him. Her parents and the rest of the family were exceedingly anxious in regard to her.

At that time, as I was on my way to Enfield, Conn., I happened to meet her father, who besought me to come around to where he lived and see his sick daughter, saying, that it was the opinion of all who saw her that she would live only a few days unless by the power of God she was raised up. I told him I could not call then, but on my way back from Campmeeting in Enfield, I would come and see her, if she was alive. I had then an appointment to preach at Palmer Depot, four or five miles from the home of the sick girl.

On arriving at Palmer, Saturday evening, I found

Bro. H. there. He had come for another daughter, who was living in P., to go home and watch with her sick sister, and see her die. I told Bro H. that after I had filled my appointment the next day, I would come and see the sick child, if she should be alive. During this time I was burdened, feeling that something was about to take place, but I could not tell what. I filled my appointment the next day, and just as the day closed with darkness I drove into the yard of Bro. H., with a burden upon me which I cannot describe. A Bro. Whitney was with me. We entered the house, passed into the sitting-room and was seated, seeing only the mother of the sick daughter and some one else of the family. We were told that stillness was necessary, as all noise affected the sick one. I inquired if we could see her. After waiting impatiently for some time we were told that she wanted to see us. I requested Bro. Whitney to go in with me. There lay the sick one, pale as death, bolstered up with pillows, the family watching as if to see her breathe her last. I passed to the bedside and said, "Ann, do you know me?" She moved her lips in assent. I said again, "Do you want to be healed; and do you believe the Lord will raise you up; and will you serve him faithfully if he will do it?" She, with all the strength she had, moved her lips again in assent.

I anointed her in the name of the Lord, and with my hands upon her head I kept repeating the promise: "And the prayer of faith shall save the sick, and the Lord shall raise him up." As I repeated this she began moving her head, and saying, "Glory," faintly. I kept repeating, "And the Lord shall raise him up." I never felt the force of this before as then. She repeated again, "Glory," but more audibly, and turned her head toward us. Her mother came to the bedside to steady her head. I said to her, "There is a stronger arm than yours holding her up, and making her whole." In a few minutes she raised her head from the pillow, and gave them to understand that she wanted to arise from the bed. Preparations were made to have her got up and dressed. Her mother brought her slippers, and in a few minutes she was on her feet, and to the astonishment of all, was walking about the room. This caused a sensation that my pen cannot describe. The parents, brother and sisters joined her and us in praising the Lord, "who had given her that soundness which caused her to stand before them whole." The contrast how great! Instead of getting watchers, and the sister coming home to see her die, she was healed, and walking about among us! In thirty minutes upon her feet, and by the power of God in answer to prayer! The Spirit of God overshadowed us. The place was a solemn one—all were greatly moved. Some in the family wanted to be prayed for, and so we had a praying season, in which all hearts were subdued. It was conviction, forgiveness, conversion, consecration. The healed one was the most conspicious in praising the Lord for his power in her behalf.

I now said to them, "It is time to retire; no one need sit up on account of Ann." They all took my advice, and there was no watching done there that night. When I came from my room in the morning, all were up, and Ann was sweeping the room where she was bolstered up in bed, almost lifeless, the evening before. She ate breakfast with us; after which we had a praise season; and then I bade them farewell. "It was the Lord's doings, and marvelous in our eyes."

NOTE.—The following articles are selected from among the many which I have written for various papers in the past years. I trust their publication here will be of service in the cause of truth and righteousness. L. B.

ENDURING TEMPTATION.

"Blessed is the man that endureth temptation: for when he is tried, he shall receive the crown of life, which the Lord hath promised to them that love him."

This is a life of temptation and trials. They come in spite of watching and good living. They come from sources least expected; they come a surprise and at a time when the enemy can make the most of it to bring discouragement to Christ's disciples and disrepute to a true religion, and so make the unbelieving think and say there is nothing in it. Hence the text gives us the necessary encouragement, and adds, "Blessed is the man that endureth temptation." It admits that the trials, the temptations, the sore spots will come. The question is not will they come? but how will you act when they do come? Blessed is he that endureth, yea, *endureth*. The man who, when the temptation comes and pinches him sore, gets vexed, and then thinks and says some hard things to or about others, is not the man to get blessings. All know we never feel better for getting mad, but always suffer loss. And as like begets like, this feeling is contagious, and others will have the same disease. As a matter of course the mind will be in a sickly condition.

Now what can be done to avert this deadly calamity? Hear the text: "Blessed is the man that *endureth* temptation." You will have it, but the remedy comes in here: "Endureth temptation." Hard pill to take, but it is the remedy, the only true prescription. It is not enough to try and bear it, though that is a great deal better than nothing, but to endure and keep sweet with the Spirit of Christ. This will bring blessings that will keep the heart from swearing vengeance, and the tongue from speaking it out. We need, yea, we must have a holiness and deep-rooted consecration from the Divine Spirit to keep us, or we shall be of no service to Christ here. It will be a threadbare profession, seen through by the spiritual eye, and which will leave us this side of the kingdom.

"Blessed." What an encouraging word. Hear it, ye disciples of the great Head of the church, "He that *endureth* to the end, the same shall be saved." Well, who then can be saved? This is a straight way; God designed it as such. He means to make it so narrow that all this rubbish of self and self-righteousness, ambition, and love of self may be forever left behind. These would be as bad as Satan in Eden and spoil the heavenly felicity. God designs that life and peace shall be eternally enjoyed in his blissful kingdom that will soon be given to those that endure to the end. Let us remember these words, and be full of courage. "Because thou hast kept the word of my patience [endured], I also will keep thee from the hour of temptation, which shall come upon all the world, to try them."

II. IS CHRIST'S COMING NEAR?

This is an important question for this generation. It is admitted the Lord will come as the Bible declares; but can anything be known as to the time of his coming? Is there any Bible evidence that the coming of the Lord draweth nigh? We answer in the affirmative. Matt. 24: 3, "And as he [Jesus] sat upon the mount of Olives, the disciples came to him, saying, Tell us, when shall these things be? and what shall be the sign of thy coming, and the end of the world?" Here is a plain question, and I think it is answered by Jesus himself. He says, "Take heed that no man deceive you. For many shall come in my name, and shall deceive many." But he tells them not to be deceived, indicating that by a close attention to what he would say they might be secure from deceptions, and their only safety was in giving heed to his unerring Word. He then put them on the track of prophecy, and marks some distinct fulfillments on the way to the end. He says, "Ye shall hear of wars and rumors of wars: see that ye be not troubled: for all these things must come to pass, but the end is not yet." Here you pass the desolation of Jerusalem, but this is not the place for Jesus' coming or the end of the world.

After this he tells us we shall come down to where

Rome will be divided and subdivided; then nation shall rise against nation and kingdom against kingdom. This must take place with famine, pestilence and earthquakes; and these are only the beginning of sorrows. These are on the track; but after the division of Rome there is to be a sad history from the persecutions which shall arise and continue devastating, betraying and killing one another. "Iniquity shall abound, the love of many shall wax cold but he that shall endure to the end, the same shall be saved. And this gospel of the kingdom shall be preached in all the world for a witness unto all nations; and then shall the end come." What end comes here? The end of the age—dispensation.

Now, then, the signs are to show when this end will come. And this gospel of the kingdom is to be preached to all nations as a witness that the coming of our Lord to establish his kingdom is nigh. The good news must be told. The nations must be apprised of the return of the Nobleman from a far country. The prophet Isaiah saw the necessity of the proclamation to be given, "Behold, the Lord hath proclaimed to the end of the world, Say ye to the daughter of Zion, Behold, thy salvation cometh"; or, "Behold, the bridegroom cometh." The message must be given; the sound must go to the end of the earth. The angel is to fly with it, for the angel with one foot on the sea and the other on the land has sworn that time shall be no longer than to give time for the voice of this seventh angel. This symbolic angel gives the signs of Christ's coming the second time, and it must be given to the generation that witnesses his advent. Then the question comes with great force, Is this the time? Is it presumption to expect and look for the Son of man at this time? We say, by the fulfillment of prophecy this is the era to have your heads uplifted; redemption is nigh.

But say some, "The Lord came at the destruction of Jerusalem." This cannot be. The Thessalonian church began to look for their coming Lord in their day, and the apostle Paul checked them in their expectations by telling them the Lord could not come till there come a falling away first, and the man of sin be revealed, the son of perdition, who "opposeth and exalteth himself above all that is called God, or that is worshiped." This is the abomination of desolation spoken of by Daniel the prophet standing where it ought not. It left a bloody track behind. Here is the tribulation, such as has not been seen before or since, and is positve proof that Jesus did not come as many suppose at the destruction of Jerusalem, from the fact that the siege at Jerusalem was in or about the year 70, and the tribulation that

Paul said must come before the Lord's coming was five hundred years this side of Jerusalem's desolation.

"Immediately after the tribulation of those days" of papal persecution, "the sun shall be darkened, and the moon shall not give her light, and the stars shall fall from heaven." Now, have these declarations had their fulfillment? They have. Immediately after the papal persecution ceased the sun was darkened, May 19th, 1780, and this is historically recognized as the "dark day." And while there has been an effort to explain it, still the fact is a mystery. God put his hand between us and the great luminary, and the sun was darkened according to his Word.

"The moon shall not give her light." The night following the "dark day" has been called by those who witnessed it the darkest night ever known. "The stars shall fall from heaven." On the 13th of November, 1833, there was the most brilliant phenomenon ever witnessed. It is fresh in the minds of many who gazed with wonder upon it.

Thus far the narration has had an exact fulfillment; and now the Master introduces a parable to enforce its application. "Now learn a parable of the fig-tree; when his branch is yet tender, and putteth forth leaves, ye know that summer is nigh: so likewise ye, when ye shall see all these things, *know* that it [or *he*] is near, even at the doors." The logical reasoning from this is that you may know equally as well when the Lord's coming is near as you may know summer is near by the putting forth of leaves. I see no way of evading it; consequently we know he is near, even at the doors. Why? Because the events have taken place in their chronological order; first, the tribulation, or bloody persecution; immediately after, the sun was darkened, the moon refused her light, the stars fell from heaven; and when we see all these things, then we know his coming is near. Then what? "Watch! for ye know not when the Son of man cometh." Watch! for "this generation shall not pass till all these things be fulfilled." "Watch! lest coming suddenly he find you sleeping."

Other signs, such as "perilous times" spoken of by Paul, and by him located in the last days, men loving pleasure more than God, "despisers of those that are good," "heady, high-minded," "having a form of godliness, but denying the power thereof;" iniquity abounding, the love of many waxing cold, commercial depression, the stagnation of all kinds of business, with the laborers crying for work or for bread, their uprising for higher wages, and their contention with monied monopolies,—all go to show that the Lord is soon coming; yea, it is just the state of things that is to precede his appearing.

They fill the mould and show him near. The rich men are beginning to fulfill what James says, "Go to now, ye rich men, weep and howl for your miseries that shall come upon you. Your riches are corrupted, and your garments are moth-eaten. Your gold and silver is cankered; . . . ye have heaped treasure together for the last days."

These are among the last signs to show Christ's appearing emphatically near. They that are ready will welcome the signs, and welcome him, and go in with him to the marriage. Then let us gird up the loins of our mind, be sober, loving, waiting, and doing all we can to save the perishing while probation lingers.

III. A TREMENDOUS LIE.

When we look back to the progenitors of the race we see that God began teaching them lessons of wisdom, so they might preserve their integrity and keep themselves out of trouble, and live among the trees and flowers of Paradise, so delightfully enchanting. He first said to them, "Of every tree of the garden thou mayest freely eat: but of the tree of knowledge of good and evil, thou shalt not eat of it." Why not? Because it was a tree which if eaten from would produce death.

Here the prohibition and the consequences are

plainly taught by God. Death was to be the consequence—"Thou shalt surely die." In their state of innocence there must be a trial to show the virtue of doing right, and the evil of doing wrong. The subtle serpent makes a call on the inmates of this beautiful place, and understanding the prohibition says to the woman, "Hath God said, Ye shall not eat of every tree of the garden?" She admitted it. The serpent said to the woman, "Ye shall not surely die." Here is the first great lie of Satan. He denied the truth of what God had said. They were tempted, yielded to the temptation, ate the forbidden fruit, were called in question, confessed their mistake and were driven from the garden, lest the fruit of the tree of life might be eaten and they live forever. For this reason the tree of life was guarded.

From that hour God's sentence of death by sin has been executed, and all have seen its workings and felt its crushing power in ending life and filling the world with tears and mourning. "It is appointed unto man once to die" is continually being fulfilled. Still the same old lie is urged upon us that men do not die, that it is an illusion; it means that they just begin to live by putting off the material and escaping with the immaterial, so that death does not kill, but is the door to life.and hastens the man to glory! You see this lie is the foundation of most of the errors of the day. The multitude side with Satan; and instead of saying, "Thou shalt surely die," they say a man does not die.

When we have learned that Satan lied, and that God told the truth, then we can see how those who fall asleep in Christ, perish without a resurrection. Let God be true if all our theories go to the winds. We shall find it safe and saving to abide by his Word, proclaim it faithfully, and abide the result.

IV. "THY KINGDOM COME."

"Thy kingdom come; thy will be done in earth, as it is in heaven," are words used by all classes of Christians more than any other Bible words. They are repeated individually, domestically, and in concert at the churches. And no fault, for Jesus said, say ye, "Our Father which art in heaven, Hallowed be thy name. Thy kingdom come." This is the model prayer, and when used we should realize what we pray for, so as to know whether our prayer is answered. "Give us this day our daily bread." That is well understood, and sadly realized when we do not receive it. Now, the kingdom,—what is it, and when will it come? We are to pray, "Thy kingdom come;" not go. I consult my Bible, whose Author gave commandment how to pray, and what to pray for. Matt. 21: 43, "Therefore I say unto you, the kingdom of God shall be taken from you, and given to a nation bringing forth the fruit thereof." Here is the kingdom of God taken from a nation, and reserved for another nation bringing forth the fruits thereof. Mark 10: 24, It is hard for a rich man to enter the kingdom of God. No drunkard, covetous, wicked or vile person can enter the kingdom of God.

Here is Bible enough to show that the kingdom of God is not the church, for some of all these classes do get into the church, and it is not hard for a rich man to find his way into the church. Neither is the kingdom of God in men's hearts, for the Bible assures us that we shall see Abraham, Isaac and Jacob in the kingdom of God. And if the Bible does not teach thus, what does it teach? We have a little promise in Luke 12: 32, which reads thus: "Fear not, little flock; for it is your Father's good pleasure to give you the kingdom." Who are the little flock the promise is made to?

An old colored man at the South was asked what that meant. He as readily replied, "Them be the good folks." Right, Jack. Well, then, the good folks are not the kingdom, but it is their Father's good pleasure that they should have it. This kingdom is their reward; this kingdom is their future home, their heaven, their paradise. Hence you hear Daniel saying: "The kingdom," "and the greatness of the kingdom under the whole heaven, shall be given to the saints of the Most High" (the little flock), and they shall inherit it forever and ever.

Now hear what Jesus says about the wheat and tares that are to grow in the field (the world), till the harvest. When is the harvest, Master? At the end of the world. What is to be done in the end of the world? The crop is to be harvested. He will "send forth his angels, and they shall gather out of his kingdom all things that offend, and them that do iniquity; and cast them into a furnace of fire: there shall be weeping and gnashing of teeth." "Then shall the righteous shine forth as the sun in the kingdom of their Father. Who hath ears to hear, let him hear." I have written this to give a glimpse of what the Lord designed by telling us how to pray and what to pray for. The earth being the territory of this kingdom, "the world to come whereof we speak," then it follows that the prayer, "Thy will be done in earth, as in heaven," involves the bringing in of God's will to be done in earth, as in heaven. That will bring heaven upon earth. When this is done the prayer, "Thy kingdom come. Thy will be done in earth, as in heaven," will be fully answered, and not before.

V. SPIRITUAL LONGEVITY.

This was published in *The Chelsea Record.*

Mr. Editor:—I had sent me the *Independent* containing a communication from the Rev. S. T. Spear, D. D., on "Spiritual Longevity," marked for my special benefit. In reading it I found that he was laboring to show that death had no effect to stay or stop spiritual or mental activity,—that death only affects the body. He says, "All the effects of death so far as known to us by observation and experience are confined exclusively to the body. We do not know enough on the subject even to presume that death involves the destruction of the soul or the suspension of its consciousness and activity for a single moment." Again, "Our higher mental faculties do not depend for their activity upon our material bodies in any such manner as to imply that the destruction of these bodies by death will be the destruction of these faculties, or any suspension of their action."

Now this seems to be a wide departure from the old primitive Bible teaching of the Puritan fathers. The received principles of Orthodox Congregationalists, as originally taught, was that there must be a day of judgment where all must appear previous to man's receiving his reward. But now it appears to be the accepted doctrine that spiritual longevity passes you right along, and that death has no effect whatever to retard its progress, as death does not affect the mental condition of men. Is this Biblical? Is it philosophical?

I have just read of Comrade Chase, who in the battle of Gettysburg was cut down by a rebel shell, his body mangled, and he carried off to the rear. On burying the dead two days after, his groans attracted the attention of grave diggers, and they found him conscious. His first words were, "Did we win the battle?" Was there a suspension of spiritual longevity here? And suppose his unconsciousness had been ten days instead of the two, would not his spiritual longevity been affected thus long? Does not this show or demonstrate that spiritual longevity is affected or stayed at death? And is not this in harmony with the teaching of the Bible? "The very day a man dies his thoughts perish."

Can a man have mental, spiritual longevity without thoughts? "For in death there is no remembrance of thee." The question is this, Does death stay, or stop the wheels of life or spiritual longevity? It is a grave question. It does seem that unperverted common sense, and the teaching of inspiration do harmonize. The Bible in its teaching seems to assume that death puts on a stay to spiritual longevity.

The apostle of the Gentiles assures us that death has ended life, longevity, unless there be a resurrection of the dead or a resuscitation to life. Is not this a resurrected longevity? And he predicates it on the fact that Jesus died, and in three days rose again, according to the Scriptures. He further says, "If there be no resurrection from the dead," "they also which are fallen asleep in Christ are perished." Could this be true if spiritual longevity was not affected by death.? Why did Jesus promise a resurrection to life if it were not necessary to his longevity? The teaching that death does not interfere with spiritual longevity seems to be nothing less than spiritualism in its present teaching. Why a judgment with all to appear, were it not necessary that rewards be rightly given? "I will raise him up at the last day." For what is he to be raised up? Is it not to give him eternal life? Eternal, mental, spiritual longevity.

VI. PASTORAL RESIGNATIONS.

I see in our paper of late many resignations of pastors. I think it a good omen for the prosperity of the Advent cause. The itinerantcy among us has done the mighty work of spreading truth and causing such a wonderful theological overturn in the world.

We are a prophetic people, raised up to spread the truth and light, in this generation; to proclaim the Lord's coming, and what he is coming for. And this is the time for these truths to be heralded everywhere. But instead of the people coming to us, we must go to them. So the work has been and still is a missionary work.

If the minister be true, and has been successful, and the people have been and still are attached to him, that is not a sufficient reason why he should stay with them. It is often when the pastor is settled, his missionary spirit wanes, and his few followers are the world to him; and then comes a loss of interest for others; so the cause languishes.

I confess there is something cheering even in resignations. It simply says, "The Lord wants me in another field." But it is all important to live so near him as to hear his voice and follow his leading. When we look for reformations, they never come out of a settled ministry. Besides, in the Advent cause there must be an aggressive missionary effort continually going on, or we lose ground. And you all know how hard it is to get young men venturesome enough to go out on the promise of God into the mission field in new places, crying, "Behold, he cometh." Money is more plenty than men, such as God can approve and prosper. Then let our churches be mission churches, and our pastors stirring missionaries, filling the land with the blissful song of redemption, and we should see a new phase of things in all our fields of labor.

I quote a few words from a good brother in his last report of mission work in New York State. He writes: "I learned long ago that when an Adventist Church ceased to be a missionary church it began to decay. If it does not make an effort to help spread abroad light and truth, it will certainly die. The same is true of the ministry."

VII. WALKING WITH GOD.

The secret of divine attainments is the "walking with God." The lack of wisdom is attributable to a not walking with God. Noah walked with God, and had this said of him: "He pleased God." Being warned of God of a coming flood, he prepared an ark to the saving of himself and family. Not only that, but he condemned the world, and became heir of the righteousness, which is by faith. How did he become an heir of God? By walking with God. Faith lighted up the pathway that God ordered him to walk in. He denied himself, walked with God, and went to work building the ark, for which he had to bear reproach and scoffing, and that kind of scoffing has come down to this day.

Would you walk with God? Is that your heart's desire? Then why not? It is the only safe way. It is the only true way. God has said in his Word, "This is the way, walk in it." Walk in it for choice, and you will be walking with God.

Enoch walked with God through a long life, and it pleased God so well that he did not let the old seventh from Adam see death, but translated him. Daniel walked with God. He refused the king's meat, and would not bow down to the golden image, neither would he stop praying with open windows, with his face towards Jerusalem. He walked with God into the den of lions, and was safe. I might go on with a great multitude of witnesses, who in the past walked with God — those that heard God speaking to them, and without a doubt obeyed his voice.

This has always been an unpopular way, or there would have been no merit in denying self to take it. But deny thyself, and take the cross, stands facing you in every turn you make while walking in the path of righteousness and obedience. It will crucify one to the world, and the world to him. Pride, popularity, worldly honor and ambition must give way, and be left behind for this gospel-shining way, that grows brighter and brighter till the perfect day.

VIII. THE PRAYER OF JESUS.

"That they all may be one in us: that the world may believe that thou hast sent me." Here is a prayer that all believers in the Lord Jesus Christ may be *one*, as he and the Father are *one*. Here is the divine requirement and pattern; and he tells us the reason for this requirement, that the world may know that the Father had sent him.

This is not a prayer for the union of sects or parties in religion, to get together in a given place and have a protracted meeting and get a hundred converts, then pull them almost to pieces to secure them to their separate folds. This is not what the Saviour prayed or wished. He says, "My sheep hear my voice; I know them, and they follow me;" consequently they are one with him, going where the Shepherd leads, having one faith, and being one company. There is no precedent in the Bible for sects in Christianity. The design was that they should be one, even as he and the Father were one. There were no Methodists, Baptists, Congregationalists, or any other "ists" in Lystra or Iconium.

The church of God, and the flock of God was one in all these places; and the apostles visited them to see how they were getting along. There were no divisions, in those days, of Christians; the pentecostal touch made them all one. These divisions are all human with their creeds to measure themselves. You may say they are Bible, but only one church can be founded on the Bible. "All Scripture is given by inspiration of God, and is profitable for doctrine, for reproof, for correction, for instruction in righteousness: that the man of God may be perfect, and throughly furnished unto all good works."

There is, therefore, no need of creeds, drawn up by men to govern the church of Christ. The voice of Christ is his gospel; and he says in that gospel, "My sheep hear my voice, and they follow me." The word of God is the creed of his church.

IX. STRIKES.

There is a peculiar state of things at present among us relative to capital and labor. New England is the oasis of the world for the workingman and mechanic. He can get more here for his work than in any other country. The most reliable men the country can boast of are the industrious, intelligent mechanics and workingmen. And while there is business prosperity, he can acquire, by his industry, position and property in accordance with his ability to occupy places of responsibility and trust.

A man, or company, investing capital and establishing a business for their own and others' benefit, should be supposed to be competent to control their own business, employ whom they choose, and pay them as they choose. For while there is competition in business, the man or the firm that pays the best wages will get the best help, and will succeed in putting the best goods into the market, thus leaving the labor problem to regulate itself to the satisfaction of all parties. For labor, like other commodities, in the market, will bring the market price. If the apples are number one they will bring the number one price, and if they are not wanted at the price, drive to the next market, and nobody's rights are invaded, law and order prevail between seller and buyer. But when you say we must take the number two apples and give the number one price or have no apples to eat, this is usurpation of human rights. Thus to see the working classes combine to force their employers, to pay prices stipulated by themselves, or be tied up is a fearful step, and will militate against the commercial interest of the country, if carried out, and inaugurate anarchy and disorder which must paralyze all business operations, and bring poverty and distress upon many.

This striking propensity of this time has a fearful outlook. The ostracising an honest laborer, willing to work for what he can get, by calling him "scab," as a mark to shoot at by the strikers, and the boycotting is pregnant with disorder, lawlessness and terror. Keep out of all these combinations, the object of which is to coerce to their demands. To have prosperity among the workingmen, who are the supporters of government, the very pith and sinew of the country, there must be a mutual interest between capital and labor, between employer and those employed, prosperity to either class cannot be had without it. It seems to me that all these strikes and overt acts of violence will paralyze and thwart the very object wished to be accomplished. I would say to my working brethren, "be swift to hear, slow to speak, slow to wrath," for wrath worketh not righteousness, or the right thing, neither the right way. Wisdom is needed in these fast times. Don't let us put hindrances or stumbling blocks in our way calculated to make the times more stringent and the workingman's prospects less prosperous. Be law abiding.

X. AND KNEW NOT.

The Lord our Maker is never faulty in what he says or does, and his plans can never be bettered by frail, human wisdom. When a plan of operation or a problem is laid down in the Bible, we may understand it to be a God-given one; that he knew what he was doing, and how it would operate; as he knew the end from the beginning. So in the days of Noah, when the earth had been filled with violence by the wickedness of men, and no other way could be devised for the good of man save his destruction; after warning and entreating him, giving him time to heed the warning and escape to a place of safety. Thus has God always done with every generation. And their salvation has and always will depend on hearing and knowing the voice of God in the fulfillment of his word.

"And knew not till the *flood* came, and took them all away, so shall also the coming of the Son of man be." Matt. 24: 39. "They knew not." Knew not what? That the flood was coming. Why did they not know? Was not the fault theirs? They had all the premonitions and signs that Noah had. The declaration of God to Noah was enough to move him with fear to the building of an ark by which he condemned the world and saved himself and family. The fault then was theirs. Had it not been, the flood would not have taken them all away. So in that case it was life to know, and destruction not to know. Noah and his family were *saved*, the rest destroyed by the flood. Why so? "And knew not till the flood came, and took them all away; so shall the coming of the Son of man be." Then, as it was before the flood, in the days of Noah, so shall it be here preceding the coming of the Son of man. This is Bible.

What does Jesus say? He says that Noah and family were saved by knowing the flood was coming; and also that all that did not know were destroyed by the deluge. And he says it will be so when he comes. Can any words make this more plain? It is terrific in its application; it is a Scripture affirmation, for it reads so, and it is so.

How is it in these days in which we live? The news of the coming Lord has been heard. The signs have been seen in the heavens; the earth has spoken, and still is speaking. The perils of the last days are being witnessed; and the signs push us to the conclusion that the Lord must soon come.

And as Noah found favor with God and was saved by knowing the flood was coming, so here, those that believe God have seen the fulfillment of his word till they *know* he is near, even at the doors. Even at the beginning of these signs they were to lift up their heads, knowing their redemption draweth nigh. You see the only difference is between believing and not believing, knowing and not knowing that the Lord is coming. "But ye, brethren, are not in darkness, that that day should overtake you as a thief."

The contrast is equally plain between the wise

servant, giving meat in due season,—which are the signs due,—and the wicked servant, saying in his heart, "My Lord delayeth his coming." One is saved in the kingdom, while the other finds his portion with hypocrites, and unbelievers. The Lord will come as predicted. What will be the result? "Unto them that look for him will he come the second time without sin unto salvation." How about those that do not look? "The flood came, and took them all away." The Lord comes. No hiding-place. They are driven away like the chaff of the summer threshing-floor. No place found for them. Thus shall the coming of the *Lord* be.

I ask, is not this a legitimate conclusion? Is not the argument conclusive? Can any other deduction be made out of the plain testimony of his Son who has spoken to us in these last days. If this is so, then there is a mighty responsiblity resting on this generation, to whom God has committed this crowning message of the Coming One. If it is suppertime, the people must be invited. They would have excuse if not invited. But when invited and told it is supper-time, then no excuse can be made. When I see little or no importance put upon this last message, given to this generation, the last one that will ever offer salvation through the only Son of God, I want all to be awake to the importance of being in the light. When we that *preach* begin to be indifferent, and put "not knowing" instead of knowing, and that it is but little matter, only try and save some, I think even now blindness in part has happened to Advent Israel. May the Lord anoint our eyes with eye-salve, that we see the signs that assure the coming of our Lord in this generation. Salvation depends upon knowing the time of our visitation.

XI. "REVEREND."

Carelessness often gets us out of the way of strict obedience to the divine commands, and leads to the use of means and measures and also *names* that are unscriptural and unbecoming in an educated Christian person, and should be strenuously avoided by those who desire to walk in due humility after their pattern, the Son of God, and also the apostles. The exaltation of man and the receiving of undue honor from one another is the great sin of this age, as well as of all the ages. The application of the title "Reverend" to a preacher of the gospel is decidedly out of place. It is a title used but once in the Bible, and then in the most sacred manner: Psa. 111: 9, "He sent redemption unto his people: he hath commanded his covenant forever: holy and reverend is his name." Here the name has its right application, to the great

God, the almighty One, he who framed the worlds by his word, "so that things which are seen were not made of things which do appear." This God, who created heaven and earth out of nothing, and man out of the dust of the earth, is the one, and the only one, to whom the Bible gives the title of "reverend." Inspiration has given it the right application. It is a sacred title, belonging to none other than God. "Holy and reverend is his name." It is God's title; and is it not sacrilege to apply this divine title to any mortal man, even if he has commenced to learn the ways of God and hath found pleasure in obeying them?

This sacred appellation is above every other. The inspired apostles never assumed it. Neither early Christians nor martyrs ever permitted such a title to be appended to their names. But I see it is working its way in among us, and while none seem to be alarmed, some seem to be flattered and pleased with it. But it is an invasion upon our Bible simplicity and right.

I well remember the reproof Bro. George Storrs, the lion-hearted Abolitionist and Adventist, gave at the Anti-Bible Convention at Hartford, Ct., when he and Joseph Turner stood up manfully in defence of the Bible. In their deliberations, said the president ostentiously, "The Rev. Geo. Storrs has the floor." Said Bro. Storrs, "Not *Rev.*; my name is George Storrs. Add no such title to my name. Once in a while I am called to address a brother by that improper title, but always with conviction of an encroachment upon the divine title."

I hope this patent, divine, Bible title may not be encroached upon, or permitted to be put on these earthen vessels that are sounding the glad tidings of a soon-coming Lord. It will detract from the excellency and power of God, blight our inspiration, and tend to formalism. We hope our brethren may withstand this wrongful invasion and walk in the old paths which lead directly to the entrance of paradise. Then the Reverend, Holy One will lead us through the gate into the city, and into everlasting blessedness and glory, to go no more out forever.

XII. A TOUR IN CONNECTICUT.

At Warehouse Point I found a few
Who'er in the faith, both good and true;
With them I found it good to meet,
And preach the truth to us so sweet.

At Hartford, the old battle-field,
I found them armed with sword and shield;
With the old veterans we had a talk,
And surely they by faith can walk.
The enemy has done his best
To crush the flock, disturb their rest;

The preachers come and oft advise,
But sometimes this is not so wise.
They should be wise and harmless too;
Good fruits should follow all they do;
The flock in Christ may all be *free*,
If all the truth they do not see.
The faithful ones will love the light,
And *all* are *one* in this good fight;
The saints of God must all be *one*,
Who love to pray, "Thy kingdom come."

Sunday I came to Cheshire Street,
Where sheep and lambs together meet;
And really it is "meat" indeed
To stand by faith the flock to feed;
At venture I did draw the bow,
And very soon the tears did flow.
The afternoon we thought it best
To point them to their promised rest;
And hearts were light and of good cheer,
To know redemption was so near.
The careless sinner, too, was there,
And in these glories wished to share;
Repent, believe, and look away
To Christ, who is the living way.

At Yalesville in the evening meet,
A gathering large of chaff and wheat;
Of new recruits here are a few,
Inquiring some, "What shall we do?"
They were pointed to the mercy-seat,
To Jesus Christ, the sure "retreat,"
To run for life, and pay the cost,
Or very soon they would be lost.
The soldiers joyfully look for peace,
And hope that soon they'll have release.
In lanes and hedges to compel,
It is our work "good news" to tell.

XIII. CARE OF THE WATCHMEN.

In this I will show how the Lord took care of his watchmen who flew through "the midst of heaven, having this everlasting gospel to preach, . . . saying with a loud voice, Fear God, and give glory to him; for the hour of his judgment is come." The call was so sudden and imperative that there was no time for systematizing their work. It was itinerancy to the fullest extent. This gospel of the kingdom *must* be preached; and the "woe" being on you, go you must, and go you *wanted* to, be it ever so self-denying. So all the watching you had to do was to perceive the opening, and earnestly step in, not knowing what would befall, save that we soon found scoffs, clubs, harness cutting, taking out linchpins, carriage wheels taken off, and such like. Other salaries were lost sight of. The gospel was not to be made merchandise of; freely as ye have received, so freely give—the poor must have this gospel preached to them.

At one place where I was giving this "message" the Lord worked, and the devil was angry and set his workers after us. They came into our meeting, and while I was speaking some of them stepped up behind me, and the brethren thought they were about to strike me. They came nigh enough to reach my

Bible and shut the book, saying if I did not "shut up" they would "knock my teeth out." But I kept the truth going without any fear, and did not lose a tooth. There was a Justice of the Peace present, and he made some effort to get the leader, but he put himself out of sight, and went to parts unknown. But this was nothing strange for those days. The old Methodist "ditty" came to our people with much force at that time—

> "The more of brickbats and of mud,
> The more of glory and of God."

I was at a certain place with Bro. Preble holding meetings certain days. Truth took effect, sinners cried for mercy, some coming to Jesus. This made a stir with the haters of the truth, and they thought they could do something to stop the work. Finally, as their last resort, they came into the meeting after we had commenced, went to the stove apparently to warm themselves, but soon went quietly out. We soon found by the sneezing and coughing that the *hot stove* had taken a large dose of Thompsonian medicine, highly impregnated with capsicum; but by the hoisting of windows the effect soon passed off, and it only gave ease and vitality to gospel breathing, and impulse to the cause. The hall was filled and we had a successful wind-up, with the fact of more than thirty-fold in converts.

These were the early days of Adventism. It was the call to supper. It was supper-time. We were told to say, All things are now ready. This was the invitation: "*Come!* the supper is waiting. *Come quickly!*" We urged an immediate compliance with this invitation. The woe was upon the watchmen then. They saw the sword coming; no time for consultation about a collegiate education, or the remuneration to be had; but the good tidings in the mouth of the flying angel must be sounded, and the warning given. "If the watchmen see the sword coming, and fail to warn, then the blood of the unsaved will be found in their skirts." This stimulated to action.

XIV. RETROSPECT OF FORTY YEARS.

The fulfillment of prophecy gives us the signs of Jesus' coming and the end of the world. In taking a retrospect of forty years, comparing the past with the present, we can see that a wonderful change has been wrought which none but God and his Word, by the power of the Holy Spirit could bring about. Literalism has stepped to the front, claiming its rights, and it has overthrown the traditions of the later Fathers, and brought many errors to a standstill. These Anti-Bible doctrines, the natural immortality of man, eternal torment in misery, the probation, or salvation of men after death, the conversion of the world, with a multitude of other spiritualizing errors, are all fading and disappearing before the blazing sunlight of the divine word spoken by prophets, apostles, and Jesus Christ. A complete return to Bible teaching has been the experience of this people while in their wanderings through the wilderness these more than two score years. Their faith has been scattered to the ends of the world.

I am glad I have had my lot with this people, marching to the heavenly orders of the Great King. Bible truth sanctifies, its sets apart by self-denial, its makes holy, it Christianizes, and cries out, "Leave all for Christ." I am glad of a place among those who cry, "Behold, he cometh!" The "ministering spirits" have been interested in this sweet gospel message, and have been sent from heaven to help us on. How often they have inspired us with the boldness of Peter and John, and for the same reason. And there has been a mighty looking on with the same confession, "They have been with Jesus." The Spirit of God made up the deficiency. To him be all the glory. The work is his. It is a thing to be coveted, working in harmony with Christ among these last crowning events. It is grand to live where a year's history of rushing events is crowded into a week.

My heart and hand is in this closing work of urging men to this last supper. This mission work is blessed. I hear the call, I see the work, and the responsibility of not giving heed to the urgent cry. But I cannot respond as formerly. Here is my trial, and it is a sore one. But my trust is in the Lord, whom I shall continue to serve, and I shall hold fast to him who has been a present help in every emergency in the past. I have no idea he will leave me comfortless on the last end of this warfare. The soldiers will not be left by our Commander if the flesh is weak on account of labor performed, or injury received while loyal to the government. So be of good cheer. We'll wait a little while, then we'll sing the new song.

XV. APOSTASY.

It seems almost impossible to keep out of this destructive channel. There is such an inbred tendency in this direction, that, unless we perseveringly guard against it, we are gliding down stream before we know it. This is so individually and collectively, —religiously and politically. It has never been known in any age that a religious body, having apostatized, ever reformed itself; but, following worldly policy, have grown more corrupt. And the only safety from utter ruin is to leave the dying carcass—"come out of her." This is done by keeping in the light which enables us to go forward.

In spite of everything that hinders, we have left the policy-seekers and world-pleasers far behind. The coming of our Lord Jesus Christ in this generation has been our cry. This was our God-given message,—this was our peculiar work,—this our preaching,—*the Coming One*. It must be stamped on all our periodicals, and written on and in all our books and tracts. It must be foremost and uppermost. All understand what "Advent believer," *Advent Herald*, *Advent Messenger*, "Advent preaching," "Advent Campmeeting," and "Advent Conference" mean. What was expected at these meetings?—in these books, tracts and periodicals? The coming of the precious Saviour, to reward every man, was made to stand out *prominent*, second to no other truth, however important. Notwithstanding the sacredness of our calling and message, with the accumulating evidence that we are in the "quickly," with the mighty responsibility of holding the awful certainty still higher, and letting the light shine, the careful watcher can see a letting down of the standard,—conservatism creeping in,—the curative medicine diluted,—sugar-coated pills given,—improved names for the heading of papers, our churches, our chapels, and our meetings. Independent, Evangelical, Christian, and any name, is better than that significant, stigmatized name, *"Second Advent."* The change seems to say, "We'll now wipe off reproach and be somebody." Thus the Lord's coming is made of secondary importance—kept in the background. These things ought not so to be. Is this standing up for Jesus? Is this the way to prepare ourselves or others for Christ's speedy coming? Is this the way to bear reproach for Jesus?

Dear brethren, raise the standard that is trailing in the dust. Welcome all the reproach that comes from keeping our old colors high, so that they may be *seen* and *known*. If this is not done amid these last events that certify our faith, the cause will suffer, and we shall never hear it said, "Well done, good and faithful," "enter thou into the joy of thy Lord."

XVI. LIFE LIKE A DREAM.

Childhood is pleasant while we're there,
Playful under parental care;
But even here, with strong desire
To be much older, we aspire.
Youth soon finds us on the way
Looking for a brighter day;

The charms and pleasures here we meet
Don't give contentment, although sweet;
Manhood at length has been obtained,
Our expectations have not been gained;
Although our prospects may be bright,
Not satisfied even with the sight.
And still we pass to riper years,
Wav'ring between our hopes and fears;
Friendships, endearing though they be,
Last not forever as we see.
No stopping place for one to rest,
The place not reached that looks the best.
Old age at last comes creeping on,
Within the sound of childhood's song.
We now have reached the highest round,
The expected *prize* has not been found;
We now can view the elysian field;
With mingled sorrow we have to yield.
If we look forward it is with gloom,
Our days have passed their brightest noon.
We now look back to early days,
Our pleasures seen in youthful plays.
We often wish that we could share
Once more the joys of parents' care.
Memory begins to grow quite slack,
To think of names there is a lack;
But when delightful acts are seen
Of youthful days, the memory's keen.
If fourscore we have lived to be,
The pleasures of childhood we can see.
'Tis twice a *child* and once a *man*,
When you have done the best you can.
Thus life has passed just like a dream;
You *never reach* the golden stream.

XVII. A HARD CASE.

In most of my journeyings I have travelled with horse and carriage. I remember of attending an Advent Conference in Plymouth County in Oct. with Bro. Bellows, and we had a good season from day to day for a week or more. The people came from abroad to hear this gospel of our coming Lord, and we had an enjoyable time in singing, praying and working for the salvation of men. When parting and leaving, a brother, that seemed to have made some progress, urged me to call on him, if I came that way. After the meeting, I stayed in that vicinity and held meetings daily until November, and was caught in a snow-storm at the last evening meeting.

In the morning I started for home, and after eating my lunch, and feeding my horse by the wayside (finding a warm spot in the woods), I started on, not knowing where the night would find me. But I found my way was by the residence of this good brother, whose invitation came fresh to mind; and about sunset I drove to his door. He was ready to answer the bell, but seemed surprised to see me, and said, "I hardly know what to do." I, said, "Have you not room to keep me and my horse?" I saw he had a long barn, and I told him plainly that my horse had gone as far as he would that night if a place could be found for him. I felt sad to think his religious zeal had cooled off so much in ten days. His wife, whom I had never seen, came to the door and said, "Drive your horse to the barn, and come in and stay with us, for there is a meeting this evening in the neighborhood, and you must stop and go with us. I was cheered by the good woman's welcome, and stayed. Went to meeting; had a blessed good time, learned that "all was not gold that glittered." Left in the morning, paying the brother for the provender given my horse, thinking that his religion had changed materially from what it appeared to be when he urged me to call upon him at the Conference.

I have learned the difference between words and deeds—between saying and doing. "He that heareth these sayings of mine and doeth them," is the man that will stand when his Lord cometh. There is a wide gulf between him that serveth God and him that serveth him not—no affinity between them. One is led by the Spirit of God, is with him in the truth, and gives a hearty assent to the fulfillment of prophecy reaching the end, having the mind of Christ. The other neglects or rejects the plan of God to save the lost! He may seek to enter in when it is too late! No entrance! The master has risen and closed the door. The wages of sin is all he can receive, and the wages of sin is death, the eternal cessation of all the attributes of life.

XVIII. AN EYE OPENER.

In reading the many good things in our Paper, my eye caught this sentence in a brother's letter, and who has lately come into the Bible faith and blessed hope. Hear him confess it. "I feel like writing a few words for the *Crisis*. I had it sent me some time by a friend far away. I dearly love to read it. It does my soul good. Blessed be God, it has made an Adventist of me. I did not suppose one could be so ignorant as I was and live in a land of gospel preaching. But thank God, my eyes are opened."

This brother can now fully say, "Whereas I was once blind, now I see." What a contrast. Now the gospel is not fables, and fables are not the gospel, but they stand out in bold relief and are antagonistic. His eyes are opened. And what did it? The reading of the *Crisis*. The Spirit of God in the writers will have an effect upon the readers of our paper, and bring about a wonderful change.

The grand lessons of the Bible will be almost wholly new. Opened eyes will see man mortal, and Jesus Christ to bear our sins, and give immortality at his second coming. They will see immortality given only at the sounding of the last trump. Opened eyes will see the Bible a common-sense book, revealing a glorious harmony in the plan of redemption. They will find out what the soul is, and what the wages of sin is, which is death. They will soon learn that eternal death, destruction from the presence of the Lord, is not eternal life in misery, and will see by the Bible that no man gets his reward until Jesus, the rewarder, comes the second time to settle and reward men according to their works. And these open eyes will see all silent sleeping in *hades* till the waking trump calls to life by the resurrection from the dead. And in looking forward they will see the chosen of God running the shining way of obedience, with voices echoing. "The old paths, we have found them, and they reach to the golden city with gates open to receive the overcomers."

Now you that have friends whom you want to see this light that shines more brightly by believing that the Bible means as it reads, get the *Crisis* into their families. Make an effort to do it, and get them to reading. The result will be the opening of eyes. You run no risk, even if you give them the paper. It is a good investment. Try it. I have found it so.

XIX. HARD EXPERIENCE.

I call to mind an urgent request for me to go out sixty miles to disciple the religionists and all others with our faith, where there were but two or three of our belief. I hastened to the place, had meetings a week or more, and a blessed free time with the help of Jesus, John and Daniel. Some responded, and fell in love with the "message"; some found fault; none could confute the position; some conversions, demonstrating that the Lord by the Holy Spirit was with us. I left, feeling a strong assurance of faith that I had done by grace the best I could for the cause and people, riding cheerfully a sixty-mile journey home. All at once the old enemy stepped in for a set-to. Said he, "I would not do any more of this work; no good was accomplished. If there had been they would have given you more than sixty cents for your labor; and there are your wife and children—they will starve in this way; how little they cared for this truth or you." I hauled up my steed in the conflict. At length I said, "You are a *lying devil;* hold your tongue, or I will return and give them a week more of the same good news." Thus I got the victory, and he left me.

I rode on, and having an impression to turn out of my way for a little mission work, called at one of the free taverns to refresh myself and take courage. After a praying season of cheering and being cheered, as I was about to start for home, says the good sister of the house, "Don't you need something to carry home to your family? I have been thinking of you for the past week." I said, "I make known my wants to the Lord; he has taken care of me thus far, and I expect he will while I do good and trust his promises." She then gave me a bill and said, "The Lord wants me to give you that." I took it, and thanked the Lord, also the sister, drove home, found the bounty was needed, and it made us all happy, and gave us more confidence to trust the Lord in the future.

This has been the way of my itineracy for more than forty years' labor in the gospel of the kingdom. I have never known what I should get, only the "One I serve" said, "What is right I will give thee." I always heed a call from my Master, if I understand it is from him.

I was once invited to visit and preach to a well-to-do Advent congregation. Had a good time, a full house, and all seemed satisfied. They gave me a pittance for a sixty miles ride by cars, and a shower of "God bless you! Come again; we want you two or more Sundays." I said, "No, I cannot; the poor must have the gospel, and it is my pleasure to give it them." It is a great work to preach and live out this soul-saving gospel, but the practical preaching of doing as you would be done by, is the most convincing, the most powerful. "All things whatsoever ye would that men should do to you, do ye even so to them." This always tells. If you don't believe it, then try it.

XX. MY PILGRIMAGE.

Commissioned by my Lord to go,
And neither stop for rain or snow,
I have to run, leave all behind,
And preach glad tidings to mankind.
This cheering "message" they must hear:
The glorious coming King is near.
The signs that show His coming nigh,
These now are seen in earth and sky.

By day and night I preach and pray;
My work is hard for every day;
A weary pilgrim, homeward bound;
Rest surely here cannot be found.
A missionary, the world my field,
The Spirit's sword I have to wield.
I'm like a man upon the wheel,
He must go round though bad he feel;
My wife and children, home and all,
I have to leave at Master's call.
These twoscore years I've run the round,
And still upon this earth I'm found,
Beseeching men to turn and run
To Christ and pray, "Thy kingdom come!"
No salary promised, only bread

With water sure we shall be fed.
A bitter cup we have to drink,
'Tis a hard life I sometimes think;
Out in the world, no scrip nor purse,
Our friends look cold—and this is worse.
I look to Christ and then I see
One who was rich made poor for me,
I hear him say, "The birds have nests,
And foxes holes in which to rest;
The Son of man by night or day
Had nowhere here his head to lay."
My murmuring now has gone and fled;
I'll follow Christ, my living head;
I'll keep the faith and fight by grace,
And so I'll run the heavenly race.
We'll gird this gospel armor tight,
And keep the golden crown in sight.
We'll suffer on and will not fear,
The better day is almost here;
With cheering hope we'll wait and sing
The coming of our rightful King.
Pilgrims and strangers we must be,
If we would live, the kingdom see.
Sun, moon and stars do also say,
We soon shall see the blissful day.
Of other signs there is no lack;
Then we'll believe and not turn back.
And when this crowning race is run,
By grace 'twill be that we have won.
The watchmen soon their work will leave,
And their reward they will receive.
Father, be it Thy will divine,
That in Thy kingdom I may shine,
And with my Lord forever be
Clothed with His immortality.

XXI. MATERIALISM.

Many seem to be frightened with the word "materialism." What is there that should be avoided in Bible teaching? The Bible seems to be an intelligent common-sense book, and we need not be afraid of its doctrine. In looking over some articles of late in our paper, I am led to ask the following questions: Are we not all materialists? Can there be a man without being material? Was not the man God made out of the dust of the earth, material? Did the breathing of life into the man's nostrils make him less material? Was not the breath of life that God breathed into the material man all there was *in* him? Was this God-made, living man a sample of all the men that have succeeded him?

Here, then, is a material, living man, but of how many elements or parts? "Man was made upright, but he hath sought out many inventions." Is man composed of more parts than God put into his make-up? I see him made of dust [earth], and life gives him motion; and when life is gone he is the same as he was before he had it. So the wise man says, "Then shall the dust return to the earth as it was, and the spirit [life] unto God who gave it." Are not here all there was of man recognized in the Bible? Some think the moral element of man is called the soul. If so, where? Well, "The law of the Lord is perfect, converting the soul." Does not this mean the material man? When Jesus came near that sycamore tree he beheld the little tax-gatherer up among the leaves. He stopped and called out, "Zacchæus, make haste, and come down," And he visited him and converted him, and it was Zacchæus, the material, living, personal man that was converted, the one that stood up and said, "Lord, the half of my goods I give to feed the poor." Now you see the natural, converted man distributing his goods among the poor.

Was not Zacchæus the soul that was converted? Did not Paul get it right when he said, "If any man (or soul) be in Christ he is a new creature"? He himself had put off the sinful and put on the divine. And is not all recognized under the term man? And will not this living soul man be responsible for all he does in the judgment, whether good or bad? What is a man advantaged if he gain the whole world and lose himself [soul]? So *himself* is all there is, dead or alive. If life is in him, he lives; if life goes out of him, he is dead. Is not life the only animating principle, and is there anything that animates or can animate when life has returned to God who gave it? These are questions of divine import, and should be carefully considered and biblically settled.

XXII. OLD LANDMARKS.

In looking over some old papers the other day, this "war effusion" of March 7, 1863, came to the surface, and which I wrote to my wife from Kennebunkport twenty-one years since. On reading it to some friends, they requested me to send it for publication in our paper, so I consented, hoping it might be of some service to the soldiers of the cross.

I am now at Camp Mitchell, Kennebunkport;
My service is first to examine the fort,
To see if their works are thorough and right;
To see if the soldiers are ready to fight;
To see if their weapons are improved and the best;
To see if their fixings will all stand the test;
To see if they're *loyal*, and will stand to their post
If the rebels should come with a numberless host;
To see if they love their Commander, so dear,
And are ready to march in love and not fear;
To see that their rations of meat and of bread,
Are rightly dealt out and *daily* are fed;
To see if their courage is like to hold out—
If they on hard tack are sent on a scout;
To see if the pickets will watch and look out,
And tell at all times what the rebels are about;
To see if the officers are content with their pay,
When a portion to them is dealt out by the day;
To see if the hardships they will endure—
If the pension to them is only made sure.
The bounty is promised from head quarters 'tis true;
It will be received by all who go through.
No "compromise" here—the constitution is right;
At the peril of life they'll fight the good fight.
The government stands—the foundation is sure;
Long life will be certain to those who endure.
Those who "skedaddle" and do run away,
Are only poor *cowards*, will not get their pay.

> Our Leader will triumph, he'll never retreat,
> And all who are with him can never be beat.
> Soon we'll gird on the armor, and marching along,
> We'll join in the chorus of victory's song.

XXIII. THE GOOD FIGHT OF FAITH.

Truth and error are always antagonistic. But some errors are more detrimental than others. Truth is always at war with every thing that hinders its progress; so there is a warfare, and the battle must be fought, or right and truth would be lost sight of. In this warfare, although it is plain where truth lies—which side it is on—yet but few have the boldness to step out in its defense and stem the tide, making themselves of no reputation by contending for the right. This has been visible in every reform in the past, and is visible still.

How many, as divine truth is being developed to their minds and hearts, give assent? They see and know the right, and while the short contest is going on, and their help most needed, they keep still; but as soon as a little victory is achieved by the fearless ones, they throw up their hats and cry out, "See what we have accomplished!" Were it not for the few reckless ones, who have acted upon principle, regardless of consequences, error would have triumphed, and truth been lost sight of long ago. But the truth has always had, and always will have its defenders. They will be brought into reproach and contempt by the despisers of truth and right; but the God of truth and right will defend them, and they will be eulogized and praised when the fog has cleared away.

Thus has it been with all theological controversies. There is a right and a wrong side, which is settled by the one standard—the Bible. There is a restlessness visible on the part of those who contemplate the future, while their salvation is not effected by repentance toward God, and faith in our Lord Jesus Christ.

Will there be a time after death, or after the Lord comes, to secure this greatest of all prizes? These are questions of the greatest importance. And on this rock many will make shipwreck, and be forever lost! Now is the day of salvation, the day of pardon, the day of forgiveness. "How shall ye escape if ye neglect so great salvation?"

XXIV. HE THAT SHALL ENDURE TO THE END.

"Now the Spirit speaketh expressly, that in the latter times some shall depart from the faith"; and these being the latter times, or last days, we are to look well to ourselves, and to the Word of life that has been our stay thus far, and hold fast to the end; for they that "endure to the end, the same shall be saved." And this end is the end of this age, or dispensation; that is, that they endure through this generation, having had the signs of Christ's second advent, they are the ones specially referred to in this passage. To endure means to suffer for Christ's and the truth's sake. They that suffer for him shall reign with him. Can this mean less? Then having been by the voice of God summoned to the supper, and at "supper time" speaking to us by prophets, apostles, and also by his Son, in signs unmistakable, shall we be safe not to hold fast whereunto we have attained, with the assurance "for in due season we shall reap, if we faint not"?

I see the tendency of the Advent Church to deviate, little by little, from the old standard, and as they do, there is a conformity to the world, that makes one look and act as the world does; seeking the wisdom of the world for direction, and asking how other people do to accomplish their purposes and plans. This is visible. "If any lack wisdom, let him ask of God, who giveth liberally, and upbraideth not." This seems to be the last place to which they look. Their acts show they think to take care of themselves, and will not seek that wisdom that comes from above.

A preacher of the gospel should know what the Lord would have him preach, and preach it, whether the people hear or forbear. He should never inquire whether it suits the rulers or not. If we are under a God-given command, then let us so divide the word of truth as to be approved of God. And if God could so approve of this message in the past as to set his seal upon it, will he not approve of the same unflinching steadfastness now? This last message is committed to our trust, under God, and shall we be seeking for broken cisterns that can hold no water? The flock of God should demand of those whom the Holy Ghost hath made overseers, their feed in this generation. Those in the faith should require that all their publications give the certain sound, as well as sound doctrine, relative to warning the world that sudden destruction is coming upon those that corrupt the earth, while Christ is coming to save his people.

XXV. CAUTION.

The Lord has taken special care to apprise us of the great danger there would be, while we were nearing the end, of apostatizing and being lost. So he said, "The love of many shall wax cold. But he that shall endure to the end, the same shall be saved."

He also said, "Take heed to yourselves, lest at any time your hearts be overcharged with surfeiting and drunkenness, and the cares of this life, and so that day overtake you unawares." And the apostle says, "He that lacketh these things is *blind*, and cannot see afar off, and hath forgotten that he was purged from his old sins." If he had not been purged, he would not have had anything to forget. To forget the illumination by the Spirit of God, in the cleansing process of conversion must be an eternal loss of life, unless re-converted by the power of God.

This type of backsliding is more prevalent in these last days, and is often seen among us. "The Spirit speaketh expressly, that in the latter times some shall fall away from the faith." There is now a terrible backsliding from the faith. Fault finding with the brethren is the prominent feature in these times, with a lack of interest in spiritual things. The backslider's place in the prayer meeting is often vacant, and when he does come he often sits back; his voice is not heard.

These are trying times, and a developement of character is going on rapidly by the Spirit of God and the truth, so that a manifestation presents itself in spite of a caution to cover up, and every man is finally found with the company of his choice. While a man keeps himself in the love of God and the appearing of Jesus Christ; in the spirit of this gospel of the kingdom, he will not leave the cause nor his brethren. He is so linked to them by the Holy Spirit and divine love that you cannot drive him away. A little jealousy, a few words said against him, and he does not leave and run to other parties; not he. He has a *stick-to-it-iveness* that holds him to his post in tribulation; and his abiding faith keeps him, and he keeps the faith, and is sanctified, perfected, and the soon coming of Christ is the burden of his song.

I do not wonder that Jesus, seeing the apostacies of this time and of this people, who have been aroused by the signs of his coming, should say, "Nevertheless, when the Son of man cometh shall he find faith on the earth?"

"Watch and pray always." This is the motto here.

XXVI. WISDOM AT AN END—TRUTH MIGTHY.

In a certain village, just out from a certain city, was a Baptist Church in rather a "dilapidated" state, suffering from a declention. This came under the observation of a good colored preacher, whose feelings for their welfare, became enlisted, and having the woe of the gospel upon him, he went to their relief. He was a humble, whole-hearted

Christian, not much versed in scholastic learning, but just able to read that Book that makes wise unto salvation. He being full of the love of a Saviour and his plain simple word, went to them in full confidence that heaven would smile upon his labors among them. A portion of the church were of his complexion, which prejudice sets aside in many of the so-called churches of God. He toiled on, the Spirit helping his *infirmities*, and while truth, simple truth, having its effect stirred up careless sinners to turn and live, till it was fully evident that God was with this man; and seeing this, all had to confess, as in the days of Peter and John, that although unlearned, he had been with Jesus. Thus, while as he had received Christ so he was walking in him, he learned that one of those swift-winged messengers, indicated by the flying angel (Rev. 14: 6), was holding meetings at a little distance, declaring to the people the soon coming of him who was once the babe of Bethlehem, the same one that good old Simeon, after waiting for the consolation of Israel, clasped in his arms, and with eyes streaming with tears of joy, could say, "Now lettest thou thy servant depart in peace, for mine eyes have seen thy salvation."

Learning this, and being in love with this *Saviour*, the humble preacher went to hear; and as his ear caught the sound, it vibrated his whole system, and before he was aware of it, his mouth was speaking, of its own accord, "*Bless God this is it*: this is the old apostolic faith—a crown when Jesus comes—life when the chief Shepherd appears—Amen."

Like a good man, having only one interest and that with Christ, he went to his church and preached the same glad tidings, and they were joyfully received by the most devoted in the church. These shed tears of joy, and catching the joyful sound, got their heads uplifted, looking for speedy redemtion. While some were scolding the good were rejoicing with joy unspeakable, and full of glory. So our good colored brother, full of courage, moved on in harmony with the Great Teacher. Having found one fact, namely, that Jesus is really coming again, he looked still farther and asks, What is he coming for? Our brother, ready to follow the direction of Paul, "Prove all things, and hold fast that which is good," concluded to hear more about the matter. So out he went again to hear those against whom all evil was spoken. Now, astonishing to his own mind, he hears the defender of the faith, read right out of the Bible, that the saints sleep—that "they fall asleep in Jesus." And again, "If we believe that Jesus died and rose again, even so them also that sleep in Jesus will God bring with him." Thus becoming fully settled in the faith, and fearless in meekness and love, speaking the same to the church, they, to a greater or less extent, believing the same, his course began to make a stir. The church surely had outgrown their creeds, and that of their neighbors, and something must be done. So the disturbed ones concluded to have a meeting of the divines, to see if our brother could not be purged from these dangerous doctrines.

Well, the divines came together, and after due deliberation they concluded he must be questioned, and straightened up, on his theology. One of the *wise* and *learned* in Greek and Latin, and who perhaps could *say* Hebrew a little, was appointed to catechise the offender. So the scene was gravely begun, the brother put upon the stand, and questioned as to the grammatical construction of certain Bible sentences. He frankly told them he was unlearned in the schools. They wanted to know if such a verse or word was synonymous with the words of another verse named; and does this and that "synchronize." He told them again he did not know much about those *great words*, said he tried to understand the English translation in harmony with common sense, and had found that immortality could only be had by seeking for it. Getting tired of this kind of operation, as they could make nothing better by it, they then began to read the tenth of John. They at length read this verse, "My sheep hear my voice, I know them, they follow me, and I *give them eternal* LIFE." They inquired, "Do you understand this?" "Oh yes;" was his reply. "'The sheep are the saints, the good children of Jesus;—Christ knows them, and it is HE that gives them life eternal.'" "Now," said he to his wise brethren, "you can readily see that it is Christ that gives the sheep eternal life, and, if you please, tell me who gives the GOATS *eternal life?*" They were all silent—wisdom had come to an end. Neither Hebrew, Greek, nor Latin could answer the question. The godlike colored brother could stand the fiery ordeal, and come out without the smell of fire upon him, and all because he stood upon the sure foundation—the blessed Word of God.

The council had no more to say. The good man is yet preaching the truth, and they can but let him go where he pleases.

XXVII. NEW DEPARTURE.

There seems to be a growing desire manifest in the Christian world to find some way to save poor humanity other than what God has made plain in his unerring Word. The condition of salvation made plain by the Scriptures of divine truth is, "Whosoever believeth on the Son hath life." This is the only name given; this is the only provision made. "God gave his only begotten Son, that whosoever believeth on him should not perish, but have everlasting life." The only way then to secure this future life is to believe on him, have our life hid with Christ in God, that "when Christ, who is our life, shall appear, we shall appear with him in glory." I know of no other way of salvation, after man is accountable for his deeds.

There is a great deal of climbing and seeking some other way, but they don't get up high enough to see their folly and turn into wisdom's way. Hence, we have a variety of methods suggested, and most of them reject the Christ that died for us according to the Scriptures. Yea, the One that "both died, and rose and revived, that he might be Lord both of the dead and living." And as he is the way and the truth, just as long as he is Mediator or Daysman between God and us, to intercede for us as our Advocate, then at the end of this mediation salvation must cease. This is a necessary conclusion. Hence the utter futility of looking for any provision to be made for them or their friends, after death, a restitution process in the next world, to correct, reform, and restore mortal men to their true righteous dignity, and ultimately to eternal felicity. This is the only world to prepare for immortality and eternal life.

There is a wide departure and apostacy from Bible teaching, when we are continually taught from pulpit and press that death takes a man directly to his reward, while the Bible gives no man his reward till he has appeared before the judgment seat of Christ; consequently, none that fall in death can have their reward without a resurrection from the dead. So Paul says, if no resurrection, "then they also which are fallen asleep in Christ are perished." The teaching that man goes anywhere at death but into the grave (*sheol* or *hades*), is a species of Spiritualism, and without foundation in the Bible. The second coming of the Lord and a resurrection of all in their graves must be had, or man will never reach his reward or doom. Those claiming to be theologically great, teach us that good men go to heaven at death and that none die. When they, amid the tears of affliction, see their loved ones placed in the grave, declare they are somewhere else. This looks absurd. But then, it is claimed to be *evangelical*, and while we do not blame men for wanting to go to heaven, we think they must wait till Jesus comes after his people, both the living and the dead. They will all get their "laid up" crown when Paul gets his. It will be as Jesus says, "Come, ye blessed," and

"Depart, ye cursed." This has not had its fulfillment anywhere in the past, so it must be future. Jesus declares it will be when he sits "upon the throne of his glory."

XXVIII. BACK THERE.

We did not have Campmeetings to see how much money, by strict honesty and economy, we could have to think of at the end of the meeting. I well remember the last services of a Campmeeting of ten days or more in Chelmsford, Mass, at which Dr. Pierce and myself were on the Committee, where we had a free gospel, a free boarding table, with more than twenty preachers, to whom we gave every one more or less to pay their expense of coming. It was a blessed time, and in the winding up of the last service, when ready to separate, the Doctor made inquiry from the stand how many debts remained unpaid for the meeting. I said, "To the best of my knowledge we need $15." He said, "We'll not take up a collection; you that have money go and hand it to Bro. Boutelle, and the bill will be paid." They soon supplied the deficiency. I paid the bills, and came away with less than two dollars in my pocket, thanking the Lord that we had been through a Campmeeting without taking up a collection.

It was an *excelsior* meeting; faith, love, fellowship and non-resistance triumphed gloriously. One day the minister at Carlisle came over to apprise us that a few of the "baser sort" were coming over to make lively work with us at the Camp, by cutting tents and doing mischief, and wished we might be ready to guard ourselves. He had heard them talk it over and was fearful for us. I told him we would do our best to be ready, for it was no new thing for us. So I watched the comers-on. As the evening drew on, surely there appeared a company of a dozen, more or less. They looked around the ground, heard the praying, singing, hallelujahs, and at length came out to our boarding tent. I said, "Good evening, my friends; you have come to see our Camp; perhaps it's your first visit to such a place. We are glad to have the people visit us, and here is where we feed them. You have probably come some ways; now please take a seat at our table and we'll serve you speedily with hot coffee and a lunch, and you'll enjoy the meeting much better." They were soon seated and feasted, and the cup of coffee took all the *mobism* out of them. They were good hearers, returned home to C., and this minister interrogated them in the morning after their return whether there was any disturbance at the Campmeeting. They said, "No; nobody could misuse them, they use people so *kindly*." Kind words and kind acts, with hot coffee and a good lunch, will do more to quell the mob spirit and keep peace in a meeting, and out of meeting, than all the threatening of law, or "You shall," or "I *will*," that can be said. Like begets like, and if you want good neighbors, set them a *pattern*, which will work like a charm. I know it experimentally, and if you don't believe it, try it, and you will be convinced.

XXIX. NO SCARS LEFT.

With the all-healing balm, and a large portion of divine love and forgiveness, how pleasurably do we run this heavenly race, looking unto Jesus, the author and finisher of this faith. This divine love would heal all difficulties among brethren and secure a peaceful influence among all classes of people that would be hard to resist. "Have any troubled or wounded you? meet them with patience. Hasty words deepen the wound; soft language dresses it; forgiveness heals and cures it, and forgetfulness takes away the scar." How full of meaning these words are, and how unlike the common usage of the world. But they are like Jesus the Saviour, in all his teachings and examples. What a godlike pattern. His directions, believed and lived out, would sweeten life with the fruits of the Spirit, which are joy and peace, with long-suffering, gentleness, and every thing else that is good and adapted to heighten our happiness, and lead us to love our enemies enough to do them good. With this holy consecration, the brotherhood would receive love; forgiveness and fellowship would be heartily practiced.

Let a man become a new man in Christ Jesus, created in righteousness unto love and good works, a divine conversion from hatred to love, the old man put off, the new man put on, then he finds it easy to wear the yoke and carry the burden. Then Paul's words would be delightfully appropriate, "Let brotherly love continue." It is like standing beside a swift running stream and saying, Let the water continue to rush along, laughing at every obstacle that comes in its way. It must and will run. So the glorious gospel of Christ shining in you in its fullness will find vent, and its flowing spirit will sweep away the rubbish and clear the channel, purifying the atmosphere and giving a healthful air, invigorating to all who breathe it. But, suppose they say all manner of evil against you falsely; be patient, slow to speak, but quick to render good for evil. Soft words dress the wound. If it does not the first time, apply the medicine again. Add a little more forgiveness. The wound is healing; soon the cure is effected, and everlasting forgetfulness takes away the scar. The new skin is clean and healthy, with no trace left. What a remedy this. Please try it.

XXX. BEECHER DEAD.

The *Advance*, in its March number, says of Mr. Beecher: "A great life has ended; it was a great life that went out in the death of Mr. Beecher."

Surely this expresses the simple fact that when this great man's life "went out" his life ended. What went out? Life. What ended? Life. Then what? Beecher is dead. This harmonizes with God's account of the making of man: "And the Lord God formed man of the dust of the ground, and breathed into his nostrils the breath of life [or lives]; and man became a living soul." (Gen. 2: 7.) How did man become a living soul? By having the breath of life, or lives, breathed into him.

So in every case of all that die; their life goes out. When this life that God breathed into man's nostrils "goes out," he is dead. His life is ended. If it were not for provisions made by God himself, that would be the last of life, as well as the last of man. If a man's life goes out, will it come into him again? This is the vital question. If a man die, shall he live again? Not if he slip out of his shell, case, or cage, and then keeps right on living. No, this is not it. His life has "gone out." The lamp, candle, light, has gone out. No light till lighted up again. This involves a re-living *from* the *dead;* a standing up of the *dead;* a resurrection of the *dead.*

XXXI. DID JESUS DIE?

The apostle affirms that "Christ died for our sins according to the Scriptures;" and also that Christ "tasted death for every man"; and we often sing, "He gave his life for me." Now did he give his life, or his body? Jesus *died* that we might live. This seems to be plainly taught in the Bible. We hear him say, "I am he that liveth, and was dead." Now all who believe in the natural immortality of man do not believe that Jesus died, but that only his body died. Ask them, Did Jesus die? Ans. "His body died, that is all." They contend that if all of Jesus Christ *died,* and went into the grave, then we were without a God three days. This is said to be "evangelical."

How would it do to say, Jesus' body died for our sins according to the Scriptures, when the Scriptures say no such thing? The Scriptures do affirm, nine times or more, that Jesus died for all, that He gave

Himself for us. It became necessary for Jesus to have a miraculous conception—begotten by the Holy Ghost, and born of a virgin, so as to blend divinity and humanity in the Saviour.

This Saviour's soul was sorrowful, even unto death; and this Saviour died. As Jonah was in the whale's belly three days and three nights, so was the Son of man three days and three nights in the heart of the earth.

The divine Son of God must die to make an atonement for us. If naught but his body died, then we have no divine sacrifice. Could the death of the human body pay the debt? We have no divine Saviour unless a divine Saviour died for our sins according to the Scriptures. All the Bible affirmations show conclusively that *all* of Jesus, born at Bethlehem of Judea, went into the grave, and that God raised him [Jesus] from the dead the third day, according to the Scriptures. He showed himself to them openly and literally; they handled him, and were convinced it was their crucified Lord. And the same literal Jesus went up to heaven in a cloud. They saw him till the cloud received him out of sight, and the angels assured the Galileans that the same Jesus should come again in like manner. So we have the only begotten Son of God for a Saviour. God gave him to be a propitiation for our sins, and not for our sins only, but for the sins of the whole world. This seems to be a vital question and plainly answered. So we may sing, "Jesus died on Calvary's mountain, long time ago."

By the eating of the forbidden fruit, man was debarred from the tree of life, and subjected to the penalty—"Dust thou art, and unto dust shalt thou return." Being excluded from the tree of life and put under the penalty of death, made it necessary for something to be done that man might not be eternally lost. God saw the necessity and made the provision. He offers the remedy—his only begotten Son, and this Son must die and go into the grave, and be raised from the dead the third day, according to the Scriptures, to be the first fruits unto God. God raised him from the dead. "Even so them also which sleep in Jesus will God bring with him"; that is, as God raised Jesus out of death and the grave, so will he bring all the saints out of the grave at his coming, and give them life—eternal life. God's only Son *did die*. It took all of this "Unspeakable Gift" to bring this fallen, doomed race to a oneness with Christ; to redeem them from death and give them eternal life at his second coming. None but a divine Saviour could do this. We will sing, "He gave his life for me," and say, adoringly, he hath washed and saved us by his own blood.

A SERMON.

Text.—"Moreover, brethren, I declare unto you the gospel which I preached unto you, which also ye have received, and wherein ye stand; by which also ye are saved, if ye keep in memory what I preached unto you, unless ye have believed in vain."—1 Cor. xv. 1, 2.

HERE is the remedy for the healing of the sick and wounded race of men. What is it? It is the gospel of Christ. This is the curative medicine for all the sin-sick ones.

Paul, whose heart's desire and prayer to God was for the salvation of all men, says to the church in Corinth: "Moreover, brethren, I declare unto you the gospel which I preached unto you, which also ye have received and wherein ye stand; by which also ye are saved, if ye keep in memory what I preached unto you, unless ye have believed in vain."

The text contains three important considerations.

1. The gospel which was received.
2. In which they stood.
3. By which they were saved.

1. The gospel of Christ must be received, or it will do no one any good. It is like a healthful remedy, it must be partaken of to effect a cure. By the first Adam's disobedience all were made sick; but by the second Adam's obedience there is a restoration to health, and health that will continue forever. There will be no sickness when the whole man is fully restored in the resurrection. No wonder that Paul called it "the glorious gospel of the blessed God."—1. Tim. 1: 11. But the great thing is to see and feel the need of this remedy. All have a kind of blood poison, and if they don't know it, it nevertheless is there. One symptom of this disease is, they who have it don't want anything done for them—they are not aware that they are sick and dying. This is the condition of the natural man. No natural remedy will reach his case. But a remedy has been provided and offered without money and without price. It was offered to the people of Corinth, and some there received it. The gospel of Christ preached by Paul was believed by a goodly number there, and they were healed of their idolatrous sins. They found the remedy sufficient to remove the disease by which they were afflicted. The gospel had its effect upon them, as it does upon every one who receives it. It brought them out from the "horrible pit and miry clay," the dark dismal place

in which they were, sinking lower and lower to destruction and death. It placed their feet upon a firm foundation, yea, upon a rock.

2. Here, Paul tells them, they stand. They stood in the gospel. They were no longer in heathenish idolatry, bowing down to idols, and under the control of Satan. They stood up straight in the glorious gospel of Christ. It was a grand foundation upon which to stand. This is the true platform, and they who are not standing here are exposed to the errors of the wicked, and led astray into all the ways of sin. To stand in the gospel is to be free. The fetters of the law are no longer worn. The shackles of the world have been torn off. There is freedom from condemnation. The doctrines and theories of men are laid aside, and the voice of Christ alone is heard. Those who stand in the gospel of Christ are independent of all the false systems of religion in the world, and there is no danger of their being deceived while they stand in the gospel.

3. The apostle adds, "By which ye are saved, if ye keep in memory what I preached unto you, unless ye have believed in vain." So the gospel saves. Paul says in Rom. 1: 16, "I am not ashamed of the gospel of Christ; for it is the power of God unto salvation to every one that believeth." The gospel, then, is the power of God, and when preached, heard

and believed it saves. It is the only thing that is to be preached to save men. There would have been none saved in Corinth if the gospel had not been preached there. But while they heard the gospel, believed it and stood in it, they must keep it in memory in order to be saved by it. They could not be saved if they forgot what was preached to them. So now, the gospel of Christ must be kept in mind, not forgotten for a day. If we would stand in it, we must take heed—remember where and how we stand. There must be watching and praying. There must be the good fight of faith in order to hold our ground and stand, having our loins girt about with truth, and our lights burning when the Master cometh.

We have said that the gospel was a remedy for sick and dying humanity. Has it been tried? Yea, verily. Look at Saul of Tarsus, full of self-righteousness, (a disease which prevails everywhere in these days), breathing out threatenings and slaughter against the disciples of the Lord. See him on his way to Damascus with hatred in his heart toward Christ and all who had embraced his gospel. What was the remedy for his terrible complaint? Was it not the gospel that he needed to cure him of his disease? Was he brought to take that remedy? After he took the remedy his disease of self-righteousness left him, and he became an advocate of the gospel that he so much hated. He has told us that this gospel will save both Jews and Gentiles, yea, that it is a remedy for sin in all the race.

We could give a multitude of instances in which this remedy has wrought wonderful cures in these our days. It has cured the heart failure hundreds of times, cleansing the heart from all impurities, so that it beat right toward God and man. It has raised to life the dead, dead in trespasses and sins, raising them up from death to live with Christ. This remedy, when applied by faith, has healed the body. Its efficacy has been attested to by many in our own day, saving from the jaws of death the saints of God. It is Heaven's remedy, not man's. It is better than the balm of Gilead or the waters of Jordan. It heals both the outside and inside—the whole man.

Does any one doubt the power of this remedy, who has not taken it? We say to him, If you will follow the directions of the great Physician, who furnishes it free to all, you will surely find yourself healed, and made to rejoice as never before, and this salvation, by the gospel, will be yours forever and ever.

APPENDIX.

Baptism and Ordination.

SOME of the readers of my book say they do not find my baptism and ordination in it, so in this edition I have concluded to supply this deficiency.

In 1837, Elder Silas Hawley, an Abolition lecturer, came to Groton, Mass., giving us some lectures against slavery. He also by consent of the Committee who employed him, gave a course of lectures on Christian Union, which were well attended, and created a great interest in the place. On account of the revival interest, he concluded it was his duty to stay and hold meetings with us through the winter. We held meetings in a hall, which were continually crowded, and after the lecturer commenced meetings, which continued fifty days in succession, and resulted in more than a hundred converts to Christ, and Christian Union, we formed a church of Bible believers, which were called Union-ists, under his care. Elder Timothy Cole, of Lowell, labored with us in this revival. The time came when these converts must be baptized, and the time was set. This stir about baptism brought me to see that the Bible said, "Believe and be baptized;" and although I had been sprinkled in babyhood, according to Puritan usage, yet I had not received baptism not believing that immersion was the only mode. When he came to the water side, surrounded by the hundred or more converts for baptism, Elder Cole led more than half of them down into the water and baptized them, after which Elder Silas Hawley sprinkled the rest by the water side—myself among them. This was the result of Unionism in Groton. In this movement fourteen of us members of the Congregational Church asked a dismission from the Church, two of the acting deacons among the members, Cragin and Dickson. So now I had two sprinklings, which were satisfactory for the time being.

Directly succeeding this revival, Bro. Miller came to Groton and this made another stir. Then we became believers in the soon coming of our Lord. Now I began to see differently; the Bible was a new book. Believing it as it reads brought new light upon our pathway, and consequently new teaching. I soon found out I had not been baptized after all. Now in my revival and campmeeting work I was often interrogated about baptism. I directed them, eunuch like, to go down into the water.

At a campmeeting at Stow, Mass., where I was on the Committee and much interested, and in which the Lord worked mightily through the preaching by the Holy Spirit, converts began to be multiplied and asking to be baptized. I assured them that we would appoint a time, and that all that felt it his duty to improve the first opportunity. So the next afternoon I gave notice that the following day at a given time all would have the privilege of obeying their Lord in baptism. My wife came to me and said she felt it her duty to go into the water. I said, "By all means go." So at the appointed time all went to the water, having chosen Eld. Joseph Turner to officiate in the ordinance. Having arrived at the water-side, Bro. Turner gave a telling address on baptism, and when he was through I was ready to go with my wife into the sacred stream, and with others be baptized. We came out rejoicing amid the shouts of joy from campmeeting worshipers. The meeting was a success.

Ordination.—In the first years of my Advent ministery I had no time nor care for ordination. My call was imperative. My work swallowed me up in the proclamation of the most enchanting message the world had heard. The demonstration of the Lord's presence and power was doubly satisfactory to me of my divine calling. It was often suggested to me the importance of ordination, but my answer was, "Not yet."

After a while there was a call for a Conference of Adventists, at Kennebunkport. Eld. Joseph Turner and R. R. York were to be there and I was urged to be present. I consulted duty, and concluded to go. On my arrival I learned that Bro. Wm. H. Mitchell was to be set apart for the ministry, and that I must participate in the services. Finding I had never been set apart by the laying on of hands, I was urged to avail myself of this opportunity, as it would be more appropriate then to participate in the ordination service of Bro. Mitchell. So I consented, and was ordained to the gospel ministry by Elder Joseph Turner and R. R. York by the layings on of hands, Father Mitchell and Gouch assisting them. This took place at Kennebunkport, Me., May 15th, 1858. Then followed the ordination of Bro. Wm. H. Mitchell to the sacred work of preaching Christ's gospel of a soon coming kingdom, and the saving of the lost. And to the honor of our Christ we are both alive working out our *salvation*, as best we can by the grace of God given us.

EXPERIENCE.

This matter of experience I make record of to show that in this sacred work of crying, "Behold, he cometh," to judgment; the Spirit of God has been with us in mighty power, and that it went before us, as in the case of convicting the old lady of its truthfulness, even before she knew the Bible reasons. Thank God for the help of the Holy Spirit to teach, and make us feel the power of truth.

In all my movements since my call to this specific work the hand of the Lord has been visible. I had a call to go to Westmoreland, N. H., to work in protracted effort with Bro. Preble. I started by stage sleigh, and arrived at Keene before dark. Thinking I would not stay at the public house, I took my carpet bag in my hand, starting out to do some little mission work by spreading the Lord's coming, thinking some family would keep me over night. So on I went, stopping, talking and leaving tracts, to tell more than I could of the "good tidings." After a few calls I began to inquire about a lodging place for the night, and having failed to secure one, and it getting late, I made up my mind the next call I made I would not preach the Lord's coming till I had secured my lodging. So I rapped at the door of a farm house. They let me in, and I directly asked if they could keep me over night. Said an old lady spinning rolls at the wheel, "My husband will be in soon, so take a seat." He came in, and cordially gave his consent; so I laid off overcoat, and felt at home, but was still about my Lord's coming.

They soon, Yankee like, began to inquire what was my business? I told them where I came from, and the old lady, before I had time to tell of my business, said quickly, "Why, is that not near Lowell?" I said, "Yes, within fourteen miles." "Well," said she, "have you heard anything about a man by the name of Miller who is preaching that the end of the world is coming? I said "yes," and this opened my budget surely. And she continued and said, "we have a girl who went from this neighborhood to work in the Lowell factory, and she has written a letter to her friends, telling them of his preaching the Lord's coming, and the end of the world, and I have seen the letter, and ever since I read that letter I have felt that it is true. And now I want to know all about it." So this opened up an evening's talk, and it was as pleasant to me as to them.

So I began at Daniel, and rehearsed all the signs of my Lord's coming, repeating to them all the prophets, Jesus and the apostles had said concerning the glorious event; and did not our hearts burn within us and them as they heard the story for the first time?

It was blessed. The Spirit of the Lord, that convicted her of the truth by hearing that letter read, was with us to give it vitality that evening. In the morning the man of the house was so interested in the subject that he gave me fifty cents, and said he would take his horse and sleigh and carry me to the meeting, and he did, and was delighted, receiving the doctrine with gladness.

At Westmoreland we held meetings certain days, and many believed, and the power of the gospel was felt mightily, and some are alive unto this day, but many are fallen asleep in Jesus. The sound has been from shore to shore, and as in the days of Noah, few believe it. "And they knew not" because they would not; nevertheless the flood came and took them all away. "So shall the coming of the Son of man be." Awful responsibilities are resting on those that live in these days of light of the signs of the Lord's soon coming.

And now, dear reader, another year has been added to my life since I wrote the narrative of some incidents of my pilgrimage; and I am yet among the living, able to preach occasionally, enjoying good living religion, with comfortable health, waiting for the Son of man from heaven.

www.ingramcontent.com/pod-product-compliance
Lightning Source LLC
Chambersburg PA
CBHW031830230426
43669CB00009B/1293